AUTO-PILOT

PILOT

The **ART & SCIENCE**

of **DOING NOTHING**

ANDREW SMART

O/R

OR Books

New York · London

© 2013 Andrew Smart

Printed by OR Books, New York and London
Visit our website at www.orbooks.com

First printing 2013

Cataloging-in-Publication data is available from the Library of Congress.
A catalog record for this book is available from the British Library.

ISBN 978-1-939293-10-7 paperback
ISBN 978-1-939293-11-4 e-book

Typeset by Lapiz Digital, Chennai, India.
Printed by BookMobile, USA, and CPI, UK. The U.S. printed edition of this book
comes on Forest Stewardship Council-certified, 30% recycled paper. The printer,
BookMobile, is 100% wind-powered.

CONTENTS

INTRODUCTION

I have often wondered whether especially those days when we are forced to remain idle are not precisely the days spent in the most profound activity. Whether our actions themselves, even if they do not take place until later, are nothing more than the last reverberations of a vast movement that occurs within us during idle days.

In any case, it is very important to be idle with confidence, with devotion, possibly even with joy. The days when even our hands do not stir are so exceptionally quiet that it is hardly possible to raise them without hearing a whole lot.

—Rainer Maria Rilke

This book is about being idle. Being idle is one of the most important activities in life, and I have roused myself to share my thoughts on the subject, and hope to convince others as well. This, despite the fact that all over the world our working hours are increasing and every time management book on the market claims that you can and should get more done. The message of this book is the opposite. You should get less done; in fact you should be idle. Neuroscientific evidence argues that your brain needs to rest, right now. While our minds are exquisitely evolved for intense action, in order to function normally our brains also need to be idle—a lot of the time, it turns out.

We are too purposeful, too directed; we should let ourselves go on autopilot more often. In aviation, an autopilot is a system for controlling airplanes without input from pilots, developed because flying an airplane manually requires absolute, constant attention from the pilot. As flying got higher, faster, and longer, manual flying caused serious (and dangerous) levels of pilot fatigue. The introduction of autopilots allowed pilots to take a break from physically controlling the airplane so they could save mental energy for higher risk phases of the flight, like takeoff and landing. Today, autopilots use software to fly the plane.

The downside of autopilots is that sometimes pilots become confused about whether the autopilot or they themselves are flying the plane. This is called "mode confusion" and has resulted in fatal accidents.

Interestingly, your brain has an autopilot. When you enter a resting state, relinquishing "manual control" over your life, your brain's autopilot engages. The autopilot knows where you really want to go, and what you really want to do. But the only way to find out what your autopilot knows is to stop flying the plane, and let your autopilot guide you. Just as pilots become dangerously fatigued while flying airplanes manually, all of us need to take a break and let our autopilots fly our planes more of the time. The trick is to avoid "mode confusion" by taking it easy, putting away our schedule, and not getting things done.

Psychological research has shown that humans, especially American humans, tend to dread idleness. However, this research also shows that if people do not have a justification

2

for being busy, on average they would rather be idle. Our contradictory fear of being idle, together with our preference for sloth, may be a vestige from our evolutionary history. For most of our evolution, conserving energy was our number one priority because simply getting enough to eat was a monumental physical challenge. Today, survival does not require much (if any) physical exertion, so we have invented all kinds of futile busyness. Given the slightest or even a specious reason to do something, people will become busy. People with too much time on their hands tend to become unhappy or bored. Yet as we will see in this book, being idle may be the only real path toward self-knowledge. What comes into your consciousness when you are idle can often be reports from the depths of your unconscious self—and this information may not always be pleasant. Nonetheless, your brain is likely bringing it to your attention for a good reason. Through idleness, great ideas buried in your unconsciousness have the chance to enter your awareness

Our long-standing "idlephobia" has lead inexorably to our current near-obsession with busyness. In a prescient 2006 editorial in the journal *Medical Hypotheses*, Bruce Charlton argued that modern society is dominated by jobs characterized by busyness. Busyness refers to multitasking—performing many sequential jobs, and switching frequently between them on an externally imposed schedule. In most careers, the only path to advancement is through the seeming mastery of busyness. Francis Crick, who co-discovered DNA and won a Nobel Prize, famously resisted rising through the administrative ranks of the academic world because he detested managerial busyness.

The definition of idleness I explore in this book is the antithesis of busyness: perhaps doing one or two things a day, crucially on an *internally* imposed schedule. Chronic busyness is bad for your brain, and over the long-term busyness can have serious health consequences. In the short term, busyness destroys creativity, self-knowledge, emotional well-being, your ability to be social—and it can damage your cardiovascular health.

From a neuroscientific perspective, studying idleness in the lab turns out to be easy. And in fact, the incredible brain activity that only happens when you are doing nothing was discovered by accident, when subjects in brain imaging experiments just lay in the brain machines daydreaming. I extend this laboratory definition to include any time during your day that you are not on an externally imposed schedule and have the chance to really *do nothing*, or when you have the freedom to let your mind wander toward whatever it is that comes into your awareness in the absence of busyness. True insight, whether artistic or scientific, emotional or social, can really only occur in these all-too-rare idle states.

Even scientists admit that you may never really understand some of the recurring concepts of neuroscience: you just get used to them. But it is useful to be familiar with these ideas early on in this discussion, if only because they are part of your excuse for taking it easy. If you can fire off a sentence explaining your laziness such as, "I'm letting the hub of my default mode network oscillate so I can figure what I want to do with my life," people will leave you alone. And acquaintance with these concepts allows you to put many facts about the brain into some kind of a context.

Consider this a crash course in complexity theory and neural science. The human brain is a creative machine; a complex, nonlinear, natural object that has the following features:

- Nonlinearity or chaos: exponentially sensitive dependence on initial conditions. What? Most systems that engineers deal with are linear or deterministic. Most systems, even if they are nonlinear, are modeled as linear systems because it's easier (or even possible) to do the math. A linear system is one for which, given sufficient knowledge about the values of the variables that describe the system at a given time, and given sufficient knowledge about how those variables change, the future of the system can be predicted very accurately. If you "input signal" to a linear system, you know exactly what kind of "output signal" you will get. This is obviously very handy when you're trying to design a communication network, a dam, or an airplane. With a nonlinear system, on the other hand, even if you have complete information about the state of the system at a particular time, and a very good model of how the variables interact, it is impossible to predict the future of the system. This is because small changes in the initial conditions of the system can get amplified down the road and cause enormous changes to the system later on. So the further into the future you try to predict, the less accurate your predictions will be. What's more, a small input signal to a nonlinear system can cause a huge output. Or, no output at all. The best example of a nonlinear system is the weather. We can estimate how likely it is that the weather will be in a certain state in the future, and the current state of the system is a function of past states (i.e., it has a memory), but we still cannot predict its future trajectory with certainty. Fortunately for us, and unfortunately for scientists, brains are nonlinear. In nature, there are no linear systems outside the mineral world.

- Threshold: a value which, when reached, causes an excitable system to leave its normal dynamic trajectory and enter into an excited or active state. We are all familiar with thresholds in our everyday lives. A thermostat is a good example of a device that makes use of a threshold. You set the thermostat to a certain value and when the thermometer drops below that value, the heat kicks in. The value you set the thermostat at is a threshold. Neurons, by contrast, are nonlinear threshold devices. Each neuron has a threshold for firing off an action potential. A neuron has a resting state, and a threshold set by the electrical and chemical properties of each neuron. The value of a neuron's threshold changes over time. Put very crudely, signals arriving from other neurons converge on a given neuron, and when enough of those signals arrive at the right time and are of the right type, the threshold is reached and the neuron fires. The neuron then requires what is called a refractory period to recover after it has fired. In other words, there is an upper limit to how fast a neuron can spike.

- Self-organization: the spooky tendency of a nonlinear system to rearrange itself in such a way as to develop long-range temporal and spatial correlations. In other words, when you look at an ant colony what you see is the appearance of an overall structure and organization. However, each ant in the colony interacts only locally with other ants in its immediate vicinity. Each ant is oblivious to the existence of the whole colony, yet through the simple interactions of individual ants the colony emerges. It is the same with neurons. Each neuron in our brains has no idea that it is part of a brain, much less a part of "you." The key is that self-organization emerges from the system's internal dynamics without an external "teaching signal." Self-organization can only emerge from nonlinear systems. Examples include brains, societies, economies, and ant colonies. Very complicated behavior can emerge from the interaction of simple elements that make up a self-organized system. Some ant colonies have millions of members, and the colony itself displays complicated and very organized behavior. It learns over time. However each ant is a relatively simple organism following chemical trails laid down by other ants. Self-organization is why your brain and your sense of self remain nearly constant from day to day. Self-organization is also why climates are relatively stable and change very gradually. A nonlinear threshold is why even a relatively small increase in carbon dioxide might cause a huge change to the climate.

- Oscillations: any periodic or rhythmic signal. An oscillation describes the upward and downward motion of a signal like the electroencephalogram, a fan that moves back and forth, or the stock market. Single neurons oscillate, and we can measure the oscillatory activity of many neurons as the sum of electrical current in a patch of brain. One of the most striking things about neurons is that they tend to oscillate spontaneously. Oscillations at different frequencies are a key mechanism by which different regions of the brain communicate with each other, and by which neurons communicate with each other.

- Network structure: the brain has about a hundred billion neurons with an estimated two hundred trillion (yes, that says *trillion*) connections between the neurons. Try wiring a computer network with two hundred trillion connections. Despite these incomprehensibly large numbers, each neuron is only a few connections away from all the other neurons. This is because of the brain's architecture. It has been estimated that each neuron only needs to send a signal through an average of seven path lengths to reach any other neuron. This is called a "small-world" network, and it is exactly like the Kevin Bacon number, or six degrees of separation. These networks have local clusters called hubs, through which many connections pass. A few large hubs dictate much of the action. Think of the FedEx hub in Memphis—all FedEx flights fly through the Memphis hub no matter where they originate and this greatly reduces the number of connections necessary to get a package from any city in the world to any other city.

• Randomness or noise: Noise is good. This might be one of the most counter-intuitive things to understand about the brain. Noise is almost always thought of as bad or harmful, especially in man-made linear systems like telephone lines. However, in complex nonlinear systems like our brains it turns out that a certain amount of noise actually helps. Through a phenomenon called "stochastic resonance," noise in the brain controls the onset of order. Too little noise and neurons cannot pick up the signals sent from other neurons, too much noise and the neurons cannot detect the correct signals. With the right amount of noise, the brain functions normally. This noise benefit can also only occur in nonlinear systems. Put noise in a linear system and you just get noise out; put noise in a nonlinear system like a brain and you might get a symphony or a novel. Noise researcher Bart Kosko, who discovered many of the principles of stochastic resonance, calls it "the Zen of noise." We will return to the important role that noise plays in our creativity.

- Variability: every time your brain encounters something like the flashing of a simple shape on a computer screen, the neural response is slightly different. Variability in neural responses is what gives our brains the flexibility and adaptability to survive in our complex societies and environments. Because the brain is a nonlinear system, a reduction in its variability is actually the sign of pathology. During an epileptic seizure, the neurons in a patch of the brain become "hypersynchronized." That is, they lose their variability. The complete absence of variability in a brain region is what a seizure is. In Chapter 8, I make the argument that many time management approaches such as Six Sigma similarly induce organizational seizures by suppressing variability where it is most needed. In this way, Six Sigma can be thought of as an organizational pathogen.

- Synchronization: also called entrainment. While "healthy variability" is important so that the brain maintains itself in a perpetual critical state (homeostatic, but always ready and anticipating the environment), information in the brain needs to be sent. There is a competition between variability and synchronization in the brain. Roughly, and in very simple terms, it turns out that when a neuron sends a signal down an axon, over a synapse to the dendrites of the next neuron, that target neuron can only receive the signal if the two neurons are synchronized. Synchronization is when two or more coupled (a physicist's fancy word for "connected") nonlinear oscillators start to follow each other in time. This was first noticed by Dutch scientist Christian Huygens in the 18th century. The story goes that as Huygens lay in bed with a fever he watched the pendula of two clocks swinging. He noticed that after a while the pendula began swinging in the same phase together. Even when he stopped one pendulum and let it go out of phase with the other, eventually the two pendulum clocks would synchronize again. This only happened when the pendulum clocks were on the same wall because of small vibrations in the wall that were large enough to allow each rhythm to affect the other. The vibrations or noise provided the coupling mechanism between the oscillators. So it turns out that our old friend "noise" helps achieve synchronization. However, as I noted above, too much synchronization and you may get a seizure, but too little and you may not get any communication at all. And this is also yet another example of a profound scientific insight taking place while a scientist did nothing (in this case recuperating in bed from an illness).

We shall see how each of these scientific buzzwords is involved when being idle and when being creative, and why being idle might make you more creative. And each of the areas mentioned above is an active field of cutting-edge research involving thousands of scientists. There are several excellent references for further reading at the end of this book. Each topic covers whole semesters of graduate courses and for some scientists these areas are their life's work. But scientists still actually understand very little about how the brain works. What's more, applying these ideas to the study of the brain is a fairly recent development in psychology and neuroscience. So if you can gain a grasp some of these ideas and how they relate to the brain, consider yourself a person with a scientific edge.

Allowing the brain to rest opens the system to exploiting these mechanisms of nonlinearity and randomness, and amplifies the brain's natural tendency to combine percepts and memories into new concepts. Anecdotal evidence from writers and artists, as well as recent psychological studies, leads to the understanding that in order to really tap the creative potential of the brain, a complex nonlinear system, we should allow ourselves long, uninterrupted periods of idleness. At a minimum, it is possible that resting is as important for brain health as is directed mental activity, if not more important.

1

THAT LOATHSOME MONSTER IDLENESS[1]

"Be diligent in your callings, and spend no time in idleness, and perform your labours with holy minds, to the glory of God, and in obedience to his commands."

—from Richard Baxter's A Christian Directory

At least since Homer we've been ambivalent on the subject. In the *Odyssey*, the Lotus-eaters lolled around all day "munching lotus" and were both hospitable and seemingly quite content. But they were a threat to Odysseus and his crew. When he arrived at the land of the Lotus-eaters, the workaholic captain sent a couple of his men to investigate the locals. The Lotus-eaters "did them no hurt" but instead offered Odysseus's men some of their brew, which was so overpowering that the Greeks gave up all thought of returning home. Odysseus, the personification of

---

[1] Robert Hitchcock, as cited in Catharina Lis and Hugo Soly's *Worthy Efforts: Attitudes to Work and Workers in Pre-Industrial Europe* (Boston: Brill, 2012). In 1580, Hitchcock, "an Oxfordshire gentleman," proposed forming a fleet of four hundred herring boats to employ ten thousand of the poor.

the heroic CEO, forced the affected men back to the ship and then tied them to the ship's benches. He recognized that if the rest of the crew got a taste of the drug, they would never leave the island, and ordered the ship to cast off. In Samuel Butler's translation, "they took their places and smote the grey sea with their oars."

Despite the Western cliché of China as a country where work, productivity, and industry are enshrined as the greatest of ideals, during Confucian times idleness wasn't a sub-culture but an integral part of *the* culture. A Confucian gentleman grew long fingernails to prove that he did not have to work with his hands. Confucianism actually disdained hard work and instead idealized leisure and effortlessness. According to Lawrence E. Harrison, a senior research fellow at Tufts, "for the Chinese, Sisyphus is not a tragedy but a hilarious joke." Harrison writes that the highest philosophical principle of Taoism is *wu-wei*, or non-effort, which means that a truly enlightened person either spiritually or intellectually goes about life with the minimum expenditure of energy. In military matters, the ancient Chinese held that a good general forces the enemy to exhaust himself and waits for the right opportunity to attack, using the circumstances to his advantage while doing as little as possible. This is in contrast to the Western idea of trying to achieve some pre-defined objective with overwhelming effort and force. It is thus paradoxical that in spite of China's long history of embracing idleness, it's currently thought of as the world's factory. This might be because, as a Chinese physicist told me recently, China has only "overcome" Confucianism in the last half century or so.

With the coming of the Enlightenment in the West, as work became mechanized, bureaucratized, and de-humanized, philosophers fought back. At that point, as the capitalist world system started an unprecedented period of expansion, Western culture popularized the concept of the "the noble savage," one of whose particular attributes was lounging around and eating the fruit that supposedly fell into his lap. The incomparable Samuel Johnson published a series of essays on the benefits of being idle in the periodical *The Idler* from 1758 to 1760. He wrote that, "Idleness ... may be enjoyed without injury to others; and is therefore not watched like Fraud, which endangers property, or like Pride, which naturally seeks its gratifications in another's inferiority. Idleness is a silent and peaceful quality, that neither raises envy by ostentation, nor hatred by opposition; and therefore no body is busy to censure or detect it."

But the capitalists could not be stopped. The 19th century saw the advent of the global industrial economy. As human beings came to function like cogs in the complex machine called the factory, Frederick Taylor, godfather of the efficient American work ethic, introduced "scientific management" to capitalist overseers in *The Principles of Scientific Management*. His goal was to integrate the life of the worker with the life of business, by the means of what was then considered scientific understanding of humans. Taylor sought to increase production efficiency by minutely measuring the time and motion of tasks. Anticipating modern productivity fads like Six Sigma (which we will get to in Chapter 8), Taylor looked to replace each tradesman's knowledge and experience with a standardized and "scientific" technique for doing work. While Taylorism was and still is hugely popular among the business class, humanists of all stripes were unenthusiastic. In 1920, perhaps in reaction to increasing Taylorization, the concept of the robot—a fully mechanized, soulless worker, physically as well as spiritually dehumanized—was introduced by Czech playwright Karel Čapek. The very word "robot" means "worker" in Czech. The same year, American humorist Christopher Morley published his now-classic essay *On Laziness*. "The man who is really, thoroughly, and philosophically slothful," he wrote, "is the only thoroughly happy man. It is the happy man who benefits the world. The conclusion is inescapable."

Wrote Lenin of Taylor's philosophy: "... the famous Taylor system, which is so widespread in America, is famous precisely because it is the last word in reckless capitalist exploitation. One can understand why this system met with such an intense hatred and protest on the part of the workers." Despite seeing Taylorism for what it was, a new technology of exploitation, Lenin adopted many of Taylor's techniques in organizing Soviet factories.

With the advent of the 1980s and Ronald Reagan, the mantra that productivity was essential to self-esteem took hold. It was good for America, it was good for business. Laziness, on the other hand, was anti-American: as recently as 2012, the State of South Carolina used laziness as a rationale for imposing voter ID laws.[2] The lazy don't deserve to vote. In 1985, Ken Blanchard

---

[2] http://tpmmuckraker.talkingpointsmemo.com/2012/09/south_carolina_
voter_id_laziness.php?ref=fpnewsfeed

and Spencer Johnson famously tried to convince employees that "people who feel good about themselves produce good results" in the iconic *The One Minute Manager*. A watered-down spiritual parable with efficient capitalism instead of inner enlightenment as its goal, the book is about a bright young man who wants to become an effective manager. He travels the world and meets different types of managers, among them the oppressive "autocrat" and the pleasant "democrat," eventually attaining the transcendent insight that an effective manager cares about people *and* results. Eventually, the young man meets the One Minute Manager who proceeds to enlighten the young man that managerial nirvana can be reached using three simple techniques: One Minute Goals, One Minute Praisings, and One Minute Reprimands. Eventually, the young man himself becomes an ordained One Minute Manager. He becomes beloved and rich.

Still, idleness persists, despite the rise of "scientific management." Like the Lotus-eaters, modern thinkers remind us to taste the sweet fruit of leisure and take it easy. Tom Hodgkinson, editor of the annual magazine *The Idler*, wrote the UK best seller *How to Be Idle: A Loafer's Manifesto*. Tom Lutz chronicles the history of idleness in his fantastic *Doing Nothing: A History of Loafers, Loungers, Slackers, and Bums in America*. For my generation, the movie *Slacker* by Richard Linklater inspired some of us to drop out of college. A strong case for kicking back can be found in Véronique Vienne's *The Art of Doing Nothing*. Even Bertrand Russell, one of the most prolific mathematicians and philosophers of the 20th century, wrote a book called *In Praise of Idleness*. In it, he writes, "I want to say, in all seriousness, that a great deal of harm is being done in the modern world by the belief in the virtuousness of work, and that the road to happiness and prosperity lies in an organized diminution of work."

These books and many others do a remarkably good job (for often being written by self-identified lazy people) of espousing the positive aspects and importance of being idle. Some propose using idleness as just another means to success, others propose being idle simply for the sake of being idle, still others suggest using idleness as a political tool to fight the capitalist system. While I wholeheartedly endorse any reason for being idle, in this book I take the argument for being idle one step further by presenting some recent and surprising neuroscience, which shows just what your brain is doing while you are doing nothing. I make the argument (which may be contested by managers and neuroscientists alike) that doing nothing—really and truly nothing—actually makes your brain function better.

According to legend, it was while lazing in bed and staring at a fly on the ceiling that Descartes, habitually a late riser, conceived of the "X" and "Y" axes that comprise the coordinate grid, now the bane of so many grade-schoolers who lose sleep studying its properties. The greatest breakthroughs in science and the greatest works of art—in short, many of the greatest *ideas* in history—may not be the result of arduous, persistent labor. Rather, sudden flashes of insight or "Aha!" moments often come during what Rilke eloquently described as the "last reverberations of a vast movement that occurs within us during idle days." It turns out that there may be a neuroscientific explanation for this.

Rilke could not have known how spot-on his metaphorical use of the word "reverberations" would become almost a century later in modern neuroscience. As we will see, assemblies of neurons in our brains literally reverberate even while we are doing nothing. In fact, some groups of neurons in the "hubs" of our brain's many networks reverberate more intensely while we are at rest. This is a recent discovery, and one that to my knowledge has not reached a popular audience. This book is about taking the idea of reverberation seriously—and using neuroscience as the ultimate excuse for taking it easy. One of the great paradoxes of modern life is that technology, for all its advantages, is actually taking away our leisure time. We are now wired 24/7. Idleness has become an anachronism.

The "resting-state network" (RSN) or "default-mode network" (DMN), as it is called, was discovered by neuroscientist Marcus Raichle of the Washington University in St. Louis in 2001. This network comes alive when we are not doing anything. Raichle noticed that when his subjects were lying in an MRI scanner and doing the demanding cognitive tasks of his experiments, there were brain areas whose activity actually decreased. This was surprising, because it was previously suspected that during cognitive tasks brain activity should only increase, relative to another task or to a "flat baseline." This led Raichle to study what the brain was doing in between his experimental tasks. What he discovered was a specific network that increased activity when subjects seemed to disengage from the outside world. When you have to perform some tedious task in an fMRI (functional magnetic resonance imaging) experiment such as to memorize a list of words, certain areas of your brain become more active and other areas become less active. This does not seem peculiar. However, if you are just lying in the scanner with your eyes closed or staring up at the screen, brain activity does not decrease. The area of activity merely switches places. The area that deactivates during tasks becomes more active during rest. This is the resting-state network. Since then, hundreds of papers have been published examining brain activity during rest. The discovery of the default mode network has generated a great deal of excitement and controversy.

Many areas of the brain are specialized for certain functions. For example, the visual cortex processes early visual information and the amygdala generates warnings and helps us decide to fight or flee. The resting-state network is specialized for times when your brain doesn't have to worry about running from a mugger or checking your iPhone. In the absence of anything in particular to do, the resting-state network lights up and starts talking to itself (i.e., you). This network has a coherent structure in the brain, and there is little variation from person to person. The resting-state network is involved in mind-wandering or daydreaming. The resting network actually becomes active when you are lying in the grass on a sunny afternoon, when you close your eyes, or when you stare out the window at work (if you are lucky enough to have a window at work). Perhaps most interestingly, those elusive "Aha!" moments may occur more often in people who allow their brain's resting-state networks time to reverberate.

The idea of a resting-state network is a difficult thing for many experimental psychologists and neuroscientists to accept, because a foundational assumption in cognitive neuroscience is that unless you stimulate the brain with an external signal, any detectable brain activity is just noise. How can there be a coherent brain network dedicated to doing nothing? There is an ongoing controversy within psychology and neuroscience about the significance of the default mode network. The brain is viewed by some psychologists as primarily reflexive, driven only by the momentary demands of the environment.

Thus, some scientists believe that studying the brain at rest is a waste of time. Even more extreme is the assumption that brain responses to external events emerge from a so-called "flat baseline." In other words, what your brain is doing while you are doing nothing could not possibly be interesting from a scientific perspective—if you're doing nothing, your brain is doing nothing. There are many reasons why these assumptions were and still are hard to dislodge; one of the most powerful is that it is convenient to assume that everything that happens outside carefully-controlled experimental events is noise that the scientist can safely ignore. Another reason may be that most psychologists and neuroscientists tend to be resistant to ideas about brain function that originate from sources outside their fields. The default mode network fits snugly into what is called complexity theory, which we will return to in Chapter 5.

But it turns out that the brain is not just sitting there waiting for the next stimulation. Rather, the brain is perpetually and spontaneously active. It is maintaining, interpreting, responding, and predicting. In fact, the brain uses more energy for spontaneous, intrinsic activity than for accomplishing specific tasks such as multiplying eight and seven, or filling in the cells of a spreadsheet. According to renowned neuroscientist György Buzáki, professor at the Rutgers Center for Molecular and Behavioral Neuroscience, most of the brain's activity is generated from within. External inputs usually cause only minor perturbations from the brain's internally controlled program. Make no mistake: external perturbations are critical in order for the brain to develop normally. No brain can develop in isolation; the brain needs to be "calibrated" to the external world through experience. Nevertheless, the brain as a complex system keeps itself in balance through self-generated patterns. As I mentioned, the concepts behind these insights into brain function come from fields outside psychology and neuroscience, such as complex systems science and physics. We are just beginning to understand what the brain's spontaneous activity really means. We explore the resting brain and its role in creativity in more detail in Chapter 2 and Chapter 6.

What emerges, though, is the idea that perceptions, memories, associations and thoughts may need a resting mind in order to make their way through our brain and form new connections. Eastern traditions have been aware of this through meditative practices for thousands of years. In Buddhism, monks train to calm their minds. Western society has instilled in us a belief that every moment of every day must be filled with activity. Indeed, it is almost a moral obligation in the US to be as busy as possible. I will try to show that for certain things the brain likes to do (for example, coming up with creative "outside of the box" solutions) you may need to be doing very little.

When your brain is bombarded with stimuli like emails, phone calls, text messages, Facebook updates, errands, driving around, talking to your boss, checking your to-do list, etc., it is kept busy responding to what neuroscientist Scott Makeig, director of the Swartz Center for Computational Neuroscience in La Jolla, California, calls "the challenge of the moment." Clearly, it is very important to be able to respond to the moment. Sometimes our survival depends on the ability to successfully meet this challenge. However, if that moment becomes every minute of every day of every month of every year, your brain has no time left over to make novel connections between seemingly unrelated things, find patterns, and have new ideas. In other words, to be creative.

Thinkers such as Bertrand Russell, Rilke, and Oscar Wilde may have been tapping into something that is only now being revealed by modern neuroscience. Each of these thinkers, and many more, asserted throughout their lives that each person could only reach his or her potential through leisure. That may sound paradoxical; after all, we are taught from a very young age some variation of "the Devil finds work for idle hands." But given the view of our brains that is emerging from modern neuroscience, it may be no accident that as our working hours increase, our mental well-being and physical health decrease.

The human brain is unique in the animal kingdom for its ability to come up with novel solutions to problems. Animals, especially non-human primates, are certainly creative. However, they are only creative within the narrow limits of their own cognitive and perceptual worlds. Humans have invented technology to extend our perception to invisible parts of the electromagnetic spectrum, and soon we may even be able to extend our memory and cognition using neurotechnology. Many neuroscientists argue that humans are unique in the degree to which we are conscious. Humans are the only species that have created a communication system that allows us to create art and acquire complex bodies of knowledge.

We are now using our brains to try to understand our brains. Another unique thing about humans is that we can afford to be lazy because of our technology and culture. We might think that an elephant seal lounging around on a California beach is being lazy. However, nothing could be further from the truth. The seal is preserving precious body fat and energy for when he has to hunt in frigid water or avoid sharks.

How did we become convinced that idleness is evil? Idleness has always been feared in the United States. The Puritans believed that hard work was the only way to serve God. Going back to 16th-century Europe where Puritanism has its roots, Luther and Calvin both believed that constant work was ordained by God and they commanded each person to choose a job and work at it "as a century post so that he may not heedlessly wander about." Forced labor was even encouraged for the poor and unemployed as a way to keep them on "the path of righteous living."

During Luther's lifetime, Europe was urbanizing and its population expanding rapidly. This led to overcrowded cities, high unemployment, and inflation. There was an explosion in the number of urban poor in places like London, Venice, and Amsterdam. Unable to grasp macroeconomics, zealots like Luther saw the new urban poor masses as "indifferent idlers" who should be punished with toil for their original sin of laziness.

We can trace the roots of our current obsession with work and effectiveness to Luther's misperception that poverty is caused by laziness rather than complex socio-economic circumstances.[3] Idleness came to be seen as an evil. If only Luther had been trained as a sociologist, we might have more than two weeks of vacation every year.

The consequences of Luther's rabid anti-idleness philosophy, especially in the United States, are seen in our absurdly short vacations and our compulsive work ethic. (Not that the United States is alone in this obsession; the Japanese have even coined the term "karoshi," which means "death from overwork.")

The increase in working hours is also striking given the recent explosion of time management, "get-everything-done-right-now" books and seminars on the market. On Amazon, I counted over ninety-five thousand books on time management. You would need to be very skilled at time management to read

---

[3] This would be analogous to blaming the financial crisis on bankers' laziness.

all of the time management books on Amazon. Assuming the average length of a book is two hundred pages, that's nineteen million pages of time management material to read. You would have to read about three time management books a day for seventy-two years to get through them all.

If these books are really effective at making us more effective, then why are we working more hours? Why does study after study show that we are more stressed, have worse family relationships, weigh more, and are less happy because we are working too much? Does it seem odd that as the time management industry sells more books, the number of hours we work increases? To quote Bertrand Russell, "can anything more insane be imagined?"

Could it be that we just aren't getting the message? Do we need even more time management books and Six Sigma courses? That is certainly what the evangelical time management industry wants us to believe. Is it the case that if we could just get more done, we could have more time off?

On the contrary, I believe there is a fundamental contradiction underlying the relationship between our culture of time management and the number of hours that professionals work. The more effective we become, the more we are pressured to do. It is an endless cycle. It stems from our belief that time cannot be wasted under any circumstances. However, wasted time is not an absolute value like mass. You can only waste time relative to some context or goal. While you are reading this book, you are wasting time relative to your goal of getting to the store before you have to pick up your kids. In fact, from some perspective, you are always wasting time.

A scientific view of the brain is incompatible with the Lutheran or Christian view of man, and this view is also incompatible with our work ethic. The much-vaunted work ethic is, like slavery, a systematic cultural invention that resulted from a commonly held, but mistaken, idea about human beings. We look back at the slavery system now and think it ridiculous and appalling. It is clear to us now how wrongheaded the very idea of slavery was. One day, we may look back at our work ethic in much the same way. Once we correct certain errors in our beliefs about our brains, our overworked society will appear to future generations as ridiculous and appalling.

In the early 1990s, Steve Sampson, an anthropology professor of mine, was recruited as a consultant for a Danish computer company. The Danish company was hired by a company in Romania to modernize its operations. The Danes installed computers and an IT department. Everything seemed to function as planned, but a problem arose. After the computer system was activated and the employees were trained, people started leaving work at lunch time. Puzzled, the Danish managers asked why the Romanians were leaving halfway through the work day. The Romanians explained that the computers enabled them to do a whole day's work in half a day, so when they were finished with their work they went home. My professor, an anthropologist, was brought in to help solve the minor crisis that ensued. The Danes were baffled that the Romanians did not want to do twice as much work now that they had computers, and the

Romanians thought the Danes were crazy for expecting them to do twice as much work just because they could do it faster. This example illustrates a cultural gap, but also that technology such as PCs that are ostensibly supposed to give us more free time actually either reduce our leisure time or eliminate it.

Many of us read the summaries of scientific health studies that appear in popular magazines or the *New York Times*. Some of us try to implement the suggestions that researchers make about how to eat healthier, how to exercise, how to avoid cognitive decline as we age, how to educate our children, how to sleep better, how to avoid getting diabetes, how to avoid knee problems from running, etc. This book should be read similarly, as a how-to book about how to do nothing. Obviously, the "how-to" part is easy. The "why" part will take some explanation. Idleness may be a loathsome monster, but it's a monster you should get to know.

———————————

From an evolutionary perspective, going back a couple of million years, when homo sapien-like species were beginning to evolve more advanced cultures, one thing that distinguished us from the apes was the ability to plan for the future.

For example, apes are known to be proficient tool users, but they only seem to use the tools in their immediate vicinity. Chimpanzees often use nearby twigs to lure ants out of a colony. But no chimpanzees have been seen to carry a twig for miles, knowing that they might get hungry later and there might be an ant colony along the way.

The first hominid species actually started carrying tools to places where they knew the objects would be useful (as opposed to just using tools in the immediate area). This indicates that their brains had developed the capacity to represent the fact that at some point in the future they might want to eat, even though right at this moment they might not be hungry. So rather than being driven by their current state, i.e., hunger, early humans began to prepare for future states.

This necessarily requires more memory to represent the past and the future. The ability to plan for future states of hunger, cold, or thirst as opposed to just reacting to immediate desires, is perhaps what began the rapid cultural advance of human beings.

It is interesting to muse about when the concept of work coalesced in human culture. Presumably it would have been after the evolution of language. It is doubtful chimpanzees have any concept of work, but they are very social and there is some evidence that they can plan for the future to a very limited degree.

Our hominid line broke with chimps about five to seven million years ago, and something starting to resemble human culture began about 1.8 million years ago. Language is more recent. So when did "work" as something onerous and obligatory replace just being active as a function of external or internal stimuli? There must be some higher-order conscious reflection that is necessary to be able to say that you are working as opposed to doing nothing, or just trying to satisfy your hunger.

The other side of the idleness-is-good-for-the-brain coin is that our brains come with design limitations. In much the same way that James Cameron could not have made *Avatar* on one normal computer, an individual human brain can handle only so much information.

Our brains took millions of years to evolve in very different types of environments than, for example, a modern office. Humans only began reading and writing about five thousand years ago. This is why it is still such a struggle for us to learn how to read. We lack genetically specified neuronal structures for reading, and our brains have to recycle other brain structures when we learn to read. Speaking, on the other hand, evolved much earlier and we normally do not have to struggle to learn how to speak. There are stages to language acquisition that happen whenever a healthy brain develops in a language community, e.g., English, Spanish, or Chinese.

We have specialized brain structures that are attuned to speech perception and speech production. By the time we reach adolescence, we have mastered our native language without any special instructions. However, in contrast, many otherwise healthy people with normally functioning brains reach adulthood not being able to read.

I point this out because our modern way of life and our work ethic are much more recent cultural inventions than reading. Swedish neuroscientist Torkel Klingberg calls this "The Stone Age brain meeting the Information Age." For example, we do not have genetically specified brain structures for multitasking, and studies now show that multitasking makes you worse at each thing you are simultaneously attempting to do.

In a famous series of studies, Stanford professor of communication Clifford Nass wanted to find out what gives multitaskers their proclaimed abilities. Professor Nass marveled at his colleagues and friends who claimed to be expert multitaskers, people who chat with three people at a time, while answering emails and surfing the web.

In one experiment, Professor Nass showed a pair of red triangles surrounded by two, four, or six blue rectangles for a brief moment to both high multitaskers and low multitaskers (people who don't normally try to do more than one thing at a time). Then he showed the same picture again, sometimes altering the position of the red triangles.

The subjects were told to ignore the blue rectangles and to judge whether the red triangles had changed position. What he found was the low multitaskers had no problem with this task. However, the high multitaskers performed horribly. They could not ignore the blue rectangles and they could not tell if the red triangles had moved. What this means is that multitaskers cannot filter out irrelevant information because their attention is overloaded with whatever tasks they are not doing. In other words, a multitasker cannot actually distinguish between relevant and irrelevant information because the multitasker does not really know what they are doing at any given moment.

The clearest evidence of this that is an estimated two thousand six hundred deaths and three hundred thirty thousand injuries are caused each year by drivers talking on their cell phones while driving. Multitasking is compulsive behavior that actually leads to a condition very similar to adult ADHD.

Psychiatrist Edward Hallowell dubbed this condition "attention deficit trait" to describe what happens to chronic multitaskers. He also argues that the way we run our modern work environments contributes to this problem in which normally high-functioning people have difficulty organizing tasks, get easily distracted, and become absentminded. Modern information workers are interrupted on average every three minutes by instant messages, email alerts, or phone calls. It has been estimated that at work you spend anywhere from twenty-five percent to fifty percent of your day just recovering from interruptions, asking yourself "where was I?" A study by Intel found that the effects of interruptions cost them a billion dollars per year in lost productivity. Modern technology can literally make us dumber.

We can decide to become aware of our limitations and live within them. Removing such stressors makes life enjoyable, leading to a further reduction in stress. As Klingberg points out, "when we determine our limits and find an optimal balance between cognitive demand and ability … we not only achieve deep satisfaction but also develop our brain's capacity the most." This process is a positive feedback loop, which also is a feature of nonlinear systems. A big part of this process is to be idle.

Our bodies were designed for protein-rich diets and long periods of low-intensity physical activity, like walking or jogging, interspersed with idleness. Continually stretching our mental capacity beyond its limits leads to worse job performance, fatigue, and eventually chronic psychological and physical disease.

The life of a Cro-Magnon was actually more leisure than work. Back then, work was defined as hunting or gathering food. It is generally accepted that the Cro-Magnon ability to be idle led to the "creative explosion" in human evolution. In biological terms, our brains are almost identical to Cro-Magnon brains. Once basic needs are met—food, shelter, protection from elements and adversity—it is no longer necessary to work.

What follows is an exploration of what our amazing brains are doing when we are doing nothing. My goal is to offer bullet-proof scientific excuses for laziness. But I also present possible neuroscientific insights into the relationship between idleness and creativity. Finally, I hope to hammer the first nails into a coffin for the insufferable time management industry.

2

SOMEONE ELSE'S NOISE

*"Uncovering the mysteries of natural phenomena that were formerly
someone else's 'noise' is a recurring theme in science."*
—*Alfred Bedard Jr. and Thomas George*

Let us return to our resting brain. The discovery of a resting
state network in the brain is very recent. It has been likened to
the discovery of the pervasive "dark energy" in the universe.

Just as it is unsettling to imagine there may actually be a
"dark side of the force" that we know almost nothing about, it is
spooky to think our brains are doing all this stuff while we sit
and stare into space. For much of the history of modern science,
what has appeared to be noise actually represents a deeper truth
that we do not yet comprehend. In neuroscience and psychology,
the brain's spontaneous activity has been considered noise until
very recently. But it could turn out that this noise holds the key
to truly understanding our minds.

Scientists like Buzáki and Raichle estimate that as much
as ninety percent of the brain's energy is used to support

ongoing activity. This means that, regardless of what you are doing, your resting brain represents the vast majority of your brain's total energy consumption. This is also known as the brain's intrinsic activity. When you activate your default mode network by doing nothing, it becomes robust and coherent. So, somehow our brains seem to violate the second law of thermodynamics which states that left unattended, things in general get messy and lose heat. This is called entropy. It's why your kitchen just gets messier and messier the longer you don't clean it. However, the old adage that "the dishes don't do themselves" does not apply to the brain.

On the contrary, when you leave important parts of your brain unattended by relaxing in the grass on a sunny afternoon, the parts of your brain in the default mode network become more organized and engaged. In your brain, the dishes do wash themselves if you just leave them alone. It turns out your brain is never idle. In fact, it may work harder when you're not working at all.

Eventually, physicists had to accept that if our knowledge of the universe is not completely wrong, then the universe is mostly made from dark energy. Similarly, it is possible that much of the brain is being ignored by cognitive neuroscience and psychology.

Psychological brain imaging experiments are designed to test brain activation levels during specific tasks in order to find out what certain brain structures are doing during those specific tasks. I previously pointed out that an assumption in brain science is that any activity detected that is not affected by experimental manipulations is just noise. Until its existence was verified, the brain's resting state network was usually considered someone else's noise. Do not confuse this with the myth that we only use ten percent of our brains. What science has revealed is that we use all of our brains, just not in the ways many people assume.

Only minor perturbations occur in the brain's ongoing activity during a mental task like adding something to your to-do list. For example, the neural energy required to press a button whenever a red light appears in a laboratory experiment is only a small fraction (as little as 0.5 percent) of the total energy that the brain expends at any moment.

In contrast, the default mode of your brain uses a far higher percentage of your brain's total energy. Figuring out just what the brain is doing while consuming all that energy when you are spacing out is precisely what Marcus Raichle and other neuroscientists are beginning to do.

One of the striking things about our brains is that in terms of energy consumption they are as greedy as Goldman-Sachs. The brain represents about two percent of your total body weight, yet it consumes twenty percent of your body's energy. It is the biological equivalent of the one percent. In other words, your brain is a pig and it is selfish. This may be why ultra-endurance athletes can start to hallucinate after running fifty miles, or when participating in the grueling bicycle contest such as Race Across America during which cyclists ride almost non-stop from California to Maryland.

When blood sugar gets low during some insane endurance challenge, for example, and you are sleep deprived, your conscious awareness is the first thing in your body to start experiencing problems. This is true in general and especially during exercise.

Unnecessary-for-immediate-survival brain operations like having coherent thoughts are sacrificed in order for the brain to be able to maintain vital functions like respiration during a drop in glucose, electrolytes, or water. Confusion and hallucinations are also warnings from our brain that we are dangerously close to doing damage to our bodies. The next step is passing out. This is the brain's last-ditch way of protecting our bodies from exercising to death.

It doesn't always work. Every year several participants in marathons die because they inadvertently pushed their brains and bodies beyond certain critical limits. The brain will keep trying to consume its disproportionate share of your body's energy. That's why when your body runs out of energy you become a drooling zombie.

Now imagine that running yourself to death in a marathon is a compressed version of your entire life.

During the marathon, as you approach the limits of your body's capacity to withstand stress, your brain will keep giving you warnings. Your muscles will feel fatigued, and you will start to have an overwhelming urge to stop. You may become disoriented and have momentary lapses in awareness.

Some people can override these warnings and push themselves past the point of no return. Over the long term in a less intense, but no less insidious way, our brains are constantly warning us that we work far too much. On the time-scale of a lifetime, constant stress from overwork raises your risk of depression, heart-disease, stroke, and certain kinds of cancer. It's a long, horrible list.

Yet we feel obliged to risk our long-term health in order to work extremely hard at jobs we don't particularly enjoy in order to buy things we don't particularly want. This is otherwise known as free-market capitalism. According to politicians, CEOs, and bankers, this is also supposedly the highest form of social organization that human beings have attained.

Few people fear being overweight as much as they fear terrorism, even though statistically being obese is much more of a threat to your life than terrorism. We do not know how much stress and overwork contribute to shortened life-spans. But we do know that obesity and sitting all day at your desk with a low level of constant stress are related. If you knew being idle (preferably while lying down on a blanket under a tree with a nice bottle of wine) for more hours of the day could add years to your life, what would you do?

―――――――――――――――

The amazing thing about the default mode network (and the point of this book) is that its activity *increases* when we are doing nothing. What exactly does this mean? From the perspective of a brain imaging scientist using fMRI, it means that activity in this network spikes when subjects are just lying in a scanner doing nothing.

More blood is delivering oxygen to the default mode network. More glucose and other brain metabolites are being consumed by this network. And the activity in each region of the network becomes correlated. Scientists can measure how well information is flowing in your default mode network using what's called "graph theory."

Graph theory is a branch of mathematics that was invented in the 18th century. Recently, it has been remarkably useful in analyzing all kinds of complex networks, especially the brain.

Networks are made up of nodes. The nodes are connected by things called edges, which are just abstract (or physical) lines drawn between nodes. An edge between two nodes means that there is a relationship between the nodes—i.e., information can flow between these nodes. Sometimes, information can only flow in one direction. This is called a directed edge. In other cases information can flow back and forth between nodes. This is called a non-directed edge. The really useful thing about graph theory is that it can be used to study things as different as air traffic, the internet, and social networks. When parts of a system form a complex network, what matters more than their actual microscopic structure is the relationship among the parts.

In the brain, these nodes are made of anatomically distinct structures. The nodes are connected by edges which take the form of axons. Areas of the brain that are physically connected are called "structural networks." Just as the body has different parts—the heart or lungs, for example—so too does the brain. These different brain parts are connected via alien-finger-like structures called fiber pathways. The brain's structural network is dense with local clusters that are interconnected to each other and to the global network. You are likely familiar with well-known brain regions like the prefrontal cortex.

We can think of nodes as airports, and we all know hub airports: Chicago, Heathrow, or Frankfurt. These airports are huge compared to regional airports and receive much more air traffic than smaller airports. Have you ever been able to fly direct from Portland, Oregon to Columbus, Ohio? Usually you would have to fly over Chicago (or maybe even to some out-of-the-way hub like Atlanta).

The brain works the same way. There are certain structures in the brain that receive many more connections than other parts. These are the hubs. When you are idle your "brain hubs" light up with activity. More blood carrying oxygen and sugar flow to the hubs in your default mode network when you relax and start daydreaming.

Over the last twenty years, technologies like the MRI and PET (Positron Emission Tomography) have allowed scientists to look inside the living brain and take snapshots of its activity or measure how much energy certain brain parts are consuming while subjects perform experiments. We now know that each anatomically distinct brain structure is specialized to do different things.

Consider the heart. It is a specialized body part that circulates blood. Within the heart there are smaller parts and each performs a more specific function. For example, the left atrium pumps oxygenated blood to the aorta, which pumps it out to the rest of the body.

Similarly, in the brain, the prefrontal cortex is involved in so-called "high-level" cognition like reasoning, short-term memory, controlling your emotions, planning activities, and bringing relevant memories to consciousness. Another brain region called the hippocampus (parts of which are active during rest) is responsible for creating long term memories and storing them in another part of your brain called the neocortex.

The prefrontal cortex decides when it is relevant to recall certain memories or information stored in your neocortex. Each of these regions can again be subdivided into smaller sub-regions which, in concert, perform larger tasks like "remember the name of that woman who also has a child in my son's daycare and who I see every day and who knows my name."

For example, let's say you meet your Aunt Lisa. You have stored in your neocortex all kinds of information about your Aunt Lisa. This information is distributed throughout the cortex and has to be reassembled when you recall it. When you meet her, you remember that she has Basenjis, she lives in Milwaukee, and she is married to your Uncle Jim. Your prefrontal cortex helps bring all this information into your awareness because it's suddenly relevant when you're talking to your Aunt Lisa.

Conversely, any new information that you get from Aunt Lisa, including the current episode during which you met her, goes from your awareness (which involves many parts of the brain) to your hippocampus. Then if you get a good night's sleep, relax for a while, or even take a nap, the hippocampus more or less writes these new memories to your neocortex, which houses your long-term memories. This is called memory consolidation. It is especially important when you are learning new ideas or skills. So the best thing to do after learning new information is to take nap, or at least be idle.

The prefrontal cortex, the hippocampus, and parts of the neocortex have to talk to each other in order to accomplish all of this. One of the ways in which neurons and brain regions send and receive information is through synchronization of their oscillatory electrical activity. In ways we do not fully understand, when information needs to travel between nodes, this information gets coded into different frequencies which then ride on top of each other like ocean waves.

High frequency waves can only travel short distances, but low frequency can travel much farther. Thus, it appears that information coded in higher frequencies "rides" on top of lower frequencies, which can carry the information to distant brain regions. A fascinating example of perceiving far-traveling, ultra-low frequency waves was when the elephants and other animals in Thailand reacted to the approaching tsunami in 2004. Hours before any humans noticed the ultra-low frequency vibrations of the giant wave, the elephants could feel it and they headed to the hills well in advance of the destructive wave. This is because elephants can hear and feel frequencies far below the human threshold. These low frequency sound waves can travel hundreds of miles.

Human neurons typically oscillate between 0.5 Hertz and upwards of one hundred Hz. However, it seems that most of our brain's activity occurs at frequencies between one and forty Hz. The dominant frequency is called "alpha" which is around ten Hz. In the brain's networks, the node receiving information needs to be oscillating in at least partial synchrony with the node sending the information.

For example, when the prefrontal cortex needs to retrieve some associations from semantic memory, it will instantaneously synchronize its oscillations with parts of the temporal lobe, the place which stores the meanings of words. How this synchronization is achieved is still a mystery.

The precise timing and spatial extent of this synchronization forms what's known as the "neural code." This is the brain's own secret language. The holy grail of neuroscience is to crack the neural code which uses electrical and chemical signals in complex patterns that allow us to speak, read, think, remember, walk, become authors, make babies, and of course be idle.

When anatomically distinct regions of the brain collaborate, as during Aunt Lisa's visit, they temporarily form "functional networks." These networks are functional in the sense that they are only formed in order to accomplish a certain task, such as to store some new factoid from Aunt Lisa. These networks can be short-lived, only lasting a few hundred milliseconds. One unresolved question in neuroscience is whether or not temporary functional networks can alter their underlying structural networks. In other words, if air traffic going to and from Bozeman, Montana were to increase beyond this airport's capacity, would the city expand the airport, which might lead to even more air traffic?

There is evidence of large scale plasticity in musicians who, compared to non-musicians, have much larger neural structures that represent their hands and fingers in the motor cortex. But presumably these changes take place over many years of training. The same is true of bilinguals: they have extra neural structures for languages in the temporal regions of the brain. London cabbies have famously large hippocampuses, specifically in the regions that help us navigate and remember spatial locations. It's as if the brain decided to expand the airports in these areas to allow for the increased demand in traffic. It's unknown how fast this type of structural change can happen in the brain. What we do know now is that brain plasticity is possible throughout our lifespan. So it truly is never too late to learn a new instrument, to learn a new language, or to radically change your life: your brain will change, too.

As an adult, these changes may be more stressful, but they are often good for your brain's long-term health. What's also unknown is whether or not lazy people have larger or more active default mode networks. Would this be a cause or a result of being idle? If ten thousand hours of practice are needed to become an expert violinist, how many hours of being idle are required to become a master idler?

The measure of how well the nodes in your default mode network are communicating is called "functional connectivity." Functional connectivity is used to indicate how well your default mode network is working, and can provide information about your brain health in general, like the measure of how fast and safely air traffic travels between airports.

When you are at rest, fMRI data can be used to see whether the nodes in your default mode network are active together. It is possible to see if oxygen in the blood at these regions increases or decreases at the same time. If you have a healthy brain and you are at rest, you will have high functional connectivity in your default mode network. As you age, if you don't get enough sleep, if you have Alzheimer's disease, or if you've had a stroke, the functional connectivity in your brain decreases, perhaps because of damage to nodes in the network.

It follows that a lifetime of being super-productive and pointlessly-busy might also decrease the functional connectivity in your default mode network. Until Marcus Raichle discovered the default mode network, the only functional or structural networks neuroscientists thought were important were the ones they studied, which became active during tightly controlled experiments. This is because most brain scientists and psychologists assume that the brain's primary purpose is to process external information.

Until very recently, it has only been possible to study how humans respond to external stimulation. It wasn't until we developed the technology to see inside the living brain and study its activity during idleness that we discovered that most of the brain's activity is dedicated to internal operations.

This does not in any way reduce the importance of what we've learned about how different systems in the brain respond to the environment. The motor system, for example, forms and executes commands to your nerves and muscles in your limbs to carry out actions, or to react to events in the world, such as an incoming tennis serve. This system has been studied for decades. But it turns out that when the motor system engages and tells your arm to swing a tennis racket after (or actually *before*) your visual system has reported an incoming serve, it might be only using a very tiny fraction of your brain's total energy.

While it is vitally important that neuroscience discovers what it can about the motor system, it may only be scratching the surface to study discrete areas of the brain while ignoring the "noise" of the resting brain. Noise, technically speaking, is some unwanted signal that usually interferes randomly with whatever signal we are studying. But the network that Raichle observed seemed to "deactivate" during active concentration on a stimulus and did not behave randomly. Nor did it interfere with signals of interest. It behaved perfectly regularly: when a subject begins actively thinking about something, this network deactivates.

Why would a network in the brain decrease its activity during targeted mental tasks like remembering a list of words? Even more mysterious is the fact that the network decreases its activity regardless of the mental task in question. Looking at many different experimental conditions, the same thing happened: this network deactivated as soon as the subject began to perform an experimental task. Naturally, he wondered what happened to this network when people just lay there doing nothing. It turned out that the brain's noise wasn't "noise" at all.

What Raichle found so striking was that many scientists still doubt that it is possible. They argue that it's a measurement error, some technical problem, or an artifact of how fMRI data is analyzed. When subjects just lie in the MRI scanner and let their minds wander, the exact same network that deactivated during experimental tasks begins to hum with activity.

Additionally, during mind-wandering the activity in the nodes in this network becomes highly correlated. This means that each part of the default mode network behaves the same way. Crucially, the default network that activates during idleness is almost perfectly "anti-correlated" with the network that activates during tasks that require your attention. You can probably guess what an anti-correlation is: the opposite of correlation. Something "X" which is anti-correlated with "Y" means that when the value of X goes up, the value of Y goes down, and vice versa.

Using fMRI data, the signal that neuroscientists use to measure the activity of a certain brain region is called the Blood-Oxygen-Level-Dependent (BOLD) contrast. Without going into the complicated details, this signal tells you roughly how much blood and oxygen is flowing to an active brain region. When neurons increase their activity, they use more blood and oxygen (just like your muscles). A rise in the BOLD signal indicates an increase in brain activity.

Even though the network your brain uses to actively pay attention only requires a small fraction of your brain's total energy, when this attention network activates, your default mode network reduces its activity. This is what is meant by anti-correlated: when your attention network activates, your default mode deactivates. While you run around like a decapitated chicken in your daily life, trying to manage your schedule, trying to keep up with all your mobile devices, posting to your Twitter and Facebook accounts, receiving text messages, composing emails, and checking off to-do lists, you are suppressing the activity of perhaps the most important network in your brain.

The two networks I have been describing are also referred to as the "task positive network" (TPN) and the "task negative network" (TNN). The task negative network is the same as the default mode network. The task positive network is the one that becomes active when you are frantically trying to manage your time.

What all this means is that as you lie there letting your mind wander—or in the awkward language of neuroscientific writing, having Stimulus Independent Thoughts—your brain becomes *more* organized than if you are trying to concentrate on some task like color coding your Outlook calendar. Thus, when you space out, information begins to flow between the nodes in the default mode network. The activity in these regions and in the network as a whole increases. We shall see later why this might be so crucial to your creative mind, and to your health in general.

———————————

Where and what exactly is the default mode network? The default mode network arises from a set of posterior, medial, anterior medial, and lateral parietal brain regions. Posterior means "behind," medial means "middle," anterior medial means "middle front," and lateral parietal means regions that are on both sides toward the top and back of your head. The specific regions that form the default mode network are called: medial prefrontal cortex, the anterior cingulate cortex, the precuneous, the hippocampus, and the lateral parietal cortex.

What is important is to realize that these regions form nodes in the very large widespread network that is your default mode. These nodes are brain hubs. It is as if the default mode network comprises O'Hare, JFK, Heathrow, and Frankfurt airports. Together these nodes form the "epicenter" of your brain's activity.

In the back of your brain (posterior) sits the precuneous. The precuneous is a hidden brain structure because it is close to the division between your brain's hemispheres and parts of it are deep in your brain.

The precuneous has been difficult to study because of its location and because isolated injury to this region is rare. Therefore we cannot study patients who have had a stroke in the precuneous to find out what has been impaired. What we do know is that it is involved in spatial reasoning and consciousness. Interestingly, the precuneous also plays a role in self-processing operations like reflecting and maintaining a first-person perspective. Recent analysis using graph theory also indicates that the precuneous is a hub node, in addition to being part of the default mode network. Like O'Hare or Atlanta's Hartsfield Airport, it has a lot of traffic.

During experimental tasks, or in real life when your attention is directed to a PowerPoint about risk management, the precuneous shows less activity. When you are stressing at work about the slip in the project schedule or doing "deep-dives" to find out why a product failed, this region deactivates. In other words: precuneous just doesn't care.

However, the precuneous is also one of the regions that show the highest resting metabolic rate of any region in the brain. This means that at rest the precuneous starts devouring glucose like a crazed hummingbird. So if you can decouple from your "lean" workplace and start doing nothing, this hub in your default mode network revs up and starts redlining. Why is that important? The precuneous seems to be involved in self-reflection. One of the best ways to get to know yourself is to find a quiet or comfortably noisy place, stare at the sky, space out for a while and see what the precuneous gets up to.

Like the precuneous, the parietal cortex is also involved in representing you to yourself, sometimes called "meta-cognition." The ability to think about this question and to have some kind of answer comes partly from our lateral parietal cortex. Life would be pretty meaningless if you lacked any awareness of yourself.

Coherent conscious representations of our own selves may be one of the unique traits of human cognition, along with language. Does a frog know he is a frog? Our own identities are of course based on these representations. Crucially, the lateral parietal cortex allows you to know whether you are a goth, a punk, a hipster, or a brain scientist. The lateral parietal cortex is also a node in the default network and thus its activity *decreases* during externally induced mental tasks. Like the precuneous, the lateral parietal cortex is also a hub node.

This may be why as you start daydreaming at work, when you should be tracking the hours spent on the latest rollout schedule for synergizing marketing plans across business units, your thoughts invariably drift toward questions like "how did a vibrant and wonderful person like me end up doing something so stupid, meaningless, soul-crushing, and mind-numbing?" Your default mode network knows you better than anyone—including your "getting things done" self.

The next part of the default mode network, called the anterior cingulate cortex (abbreviated as ACC), requires a short digression. You know already that your brain has two halves—called hemispheres. The hemispheres are connected via a fiber tract called the corpus callosum.

The corpus callosum allows information to flow between the two hemispheres. Sometimes, this fiber tract is cut surgically to prevent seizures in people with intractable epilepsy. Sitting like a collar wrapped around the corpus callosum is the anterior cingulate cortex. It is connected to the prefrontal cortex.

One of the anterior cingulate's primary roles is to monitor your behavior together with feedback from your environment and to let you know when you've made a mistake. This is called "error detection." In a similar way, when you are idle the anterior cingulate also seems to monitor your subconscious for potential solutions to problems.

When the ACC discovers some remotely associated concepts that might work together in a novel idea it directs your attention to this idea, thus boosting its activation so that the idea can enter your consciousness. As part of the default mode network, the ACC likes it when you are taking it easy and are in a positive mood. During idleness, it appears to be ready to help you find insightful solutions and come up with creative thoughts. When you are stressed out and worried about external concerns, the activity of the ACC decreases.

Journeying to the center of the brain, we find the hippocampus. This is one of the most studied brain regions because it is what allows us to form memories. In fact, there is an academic journal devoted entirely to the study of the hippocampus, unsurprisingly if unimaginatively called *Hippocampus*.

The hippocampus is a horseshoe-shaped structure deep in the middle of the brain. It has two halves which straddle the brain's left and right hemispheres. As with all brain regions, the hippocampus seems to have a primary function—forming memories—but its sub-regions perform specialized tasks that range from learning how to navigate new spaces to creating new autobiographical memories.

When you lose parts of your hippocampus, you may not be able to create new memories. One of the reasons we know quite a lot about what the hippocampus does is from studying patients who have had parts of this region removed to stop intractable epilepsy from seizures that originate in this area. Often, when certain parts are removed, patients cannot form new memories.

So for example, when you meet a patient missing parts of the hippocampus he will not remember you the next time you meet, nor the time after that. He will not be able to recall ever meeting you before, no matter how many times you meet him.

Parts of the hippocampus which seem to be involved in the creation and retrieval of autobiographical memories are also active in the default mode network. This is why when your mind begins to wander you may start to think about riding your bike as a child, that last presentation you gave, or the maniac who accosted you on the subway this morning.

All these memories must pass through the hippocampus when they are created and recreated when you recall them. What's more, as you reflect back on your life, your default mode network seems especially good at using these memories to project forward into the future, creating images of yourself in future situations. The ability to reflect on your current situation, your past, and your future are all intimately related. People who have the luxury to spend time doing this by being idle tend to be more creative, and to have better mental health in general.

Moving toward the front of your head we arrive at the prefrontal cortex. Evolutionarily speaking, this is one of the last brain regions to evolve. Likewise, it is one of the final brain regions to mature during development. In fact, in males, the prefrontal cortex does not finish maturing until about age twenty-five. I mentioned above that the prefrontal cortex is responsible for skills like decision making, planning, impulse-control, and self-reflection—skills that many males under twenty-five tend to lack.

One of the major roles of the prefrontal cortex in your brain's cognitive life is to make information in your brain available for manipulation and action—i.e., when information arrives in your prefrontal cortex you are likely to be aware of it. The prefrontal cortex is therefore considered necessary but not sufficient for consciousness.

The prefrontal cortex is not the only source of consciousness because many brain areas have to be ignited in order for you to become aware of something. However, it seems that the prefrontal cortex must be involved for you to have any sort of meaningful human-like experience with data.

Once you have a piece of information in your awareness you can do stuff with the information—e.g., think about it, make a decision, or let it simply pass from awareness back to your unconscious, such as in meditation. The amount of information you can hold in awareness at any moment also depends on how well your prefrontal cortex is working. There seems to be a trade-off in the brain between being able to store a lot of information in your working memory and cognitive flexibility or creativity.

We often use an upside-down U-shaped curve to describe this—the bottom of one side of the U is total rigidity but very high storage, the other side of the U is complete flexibility but no storage. It turns out that being idle can help your brain naturally find a balance between these two extremes.

There are many parts to the prefrontal cortex. The region of the prefrontal cortex that is part of the default mode network is called the medial prefrontal cortex. It should not surprise you by now that this area also has a very high resting metabolic rate. There is also a high resting blood flow to the prefrontal cortex, which is critical for your conscious awareness and also for spontaneously-generated thoughts.

As part of the default mode network, the medial prefrontal cortex typically starts to shut down when you are an effective person: when you are going from your early morning gym session to the office, reviewing your PowerPoint slides, getting to the meeting, presenting the report, scarfing down take-away for lunch while checking your email, pounding another coffee, checking your calendar, putting little red dots on documents you've reviewed, answering calls, answering texts, scheduling appointments for the kids, planning to plan ... *ad infinitum.*

It is only when your thoughts drift inward does the medial prefrontal cortex start to light up and talk to its partners in idleness—the precuneous, the anterior cingulate cortex, and the lateral parietal cortex. The medial prefrontal cortex also seems to be involved in a kind of surveillance of your brain's internal operations, so that when you stop doing stuff and become idle this region of the brain can report what's going on in the deepest recesses of your mind.

In a nutshell, when you are being lazy, a huge and widespread network in your brain forms and starts sending information back and forth between these regions. The butterflies only come out to play when all is still and quiet. Any sudden movements and they scatter.

The default mode network supports self-knowledge, autobiographical memories, social and emotional processes, and creativity. It persists as long as you can relax. Remember that when you are busy checking your to-do list, making sure you paid a bill, being productive at work, or improving your time management skills, the default mode network goes dormant.

The neurons in this network fire less, and therefore these brain areas need less glucose and less blood. You may have also noticed that each of the nodes in the default mode network is involved in thinking about yourself, reflecting on the past, and introspection. What's more, these brain regions are all intricately involved in consciousness.

In addition to the disproportionate amount of energy the brain requires to maintain its ongoing activities, the structure of the brain also underlies its function of staying in a "metastable" state. "Metastable" here refers to the balance the brain must strike between stability and flexibility. In order to survive and reproduce, we need to be able to avoid predators, falling air-conditioners, and drivers talking on their cell phones.

However, it would be of little evolutionary advantage if every time we swerved to avoid a distracted driver, our personality disappeared or changed completely. In order to feel sane and make sense of the world, we need to perceive ourselves as continuous and coherent "selves." How does the brain achieve this balance between a stable state that does not change and a highly sensitive and reactive flexibility that can react in milliseconds to sudden changes in the environment?

One possibility that neuroscientists are exploring is that the actual structure of the brain, how it is anatomically arranged and organized, actually establishes this metastability. The parts of the brain that make up the default mode network seem to be critical to the maintenance of an internal representation of ourselves.

We still do not fully understand the significance of the fact that the default mode network is formed from hub nodes. Because information is distributed throughout your brain, the hubs of your brain network are crucial to the efficient flow of this information to and from your consciousness. The hub structure of your brain's network is what allows for memories to be almost instantaneously reconstructed as they enter your consciousness.

What appears to us as a single memory has to be reassembled from multiple brain regions every time we recall that memory. The short path-lengths through network hubs help this process to be so fast and automatic that we take it for granted.

In fact, recent evidence indicates that in neurodegenerative diseases such as Alzheimer's, the default node network is disrupted and shows less activation. This could be one reason why it becomes so difficult for Alzheimer's patients to recall memories: the information stored in their brains cannot make its way through the network.

Conversely, people with schizophrenia show hyperactivity and hyperconnectivity in their default mode networks. If your default mode network is too active and its nodes have too many connections, you can have problems differentiating between reality and fantasy. There is a long history to the study of the relationship between genius and madness. Many scholars have argued that there is a fine line between the two.

The fact that abnormal activity in the default mode network is involved in debilitating mental illness illustrates its critical nature. However, as with Alzheimer's disease, the disruption in default mode network activity may be a symptom rather than a cause. Between these ends of the spectrum lies an optimal level of default mode network activity which enhances our feeling of well-being, our physical health, and our creativity.

Fortunately, the only way to attain this optimal level of default mode activity is to put your feet up, find a nice pillow, lie back, and let go of task-oriented activity. Looking at great art, listening to your favorite music, and doodling may help facilitate this process.

Unfortunately, laziness is so stigmatized in America that everyone knows what it means. The trick is learning to embrace, defend, and demand the right to laziness as a prerequisite for a good life and a healthy society, and also recognizing that the astounding insights that may occur from those who have a particularly robust default mode network are not anomalies, but the norm.

3

AHA! MOMENTS AND SELF-KNOWLEDGE

"On 15 April 1726 I paid a visit to Sir Isaac at his lodgings in Orbels buildings in Kensington, dined with him and spent the whole day with him alone … After dinner, the weather being warm, we went into the garden and drank tea, under the shade of some apple trees, only he and myself. Amidst other discourse, he told me, he was just in the same situation, as when formerly, the notion of gravitation came into his mind. It was occasion'd by the fall of an apple, as he sat in a contemplative mood."

—*William Stuckley*

"A genius is someone who discovers that the stone that falls and the moon that doesn't fall represent one and the same phenomenon."
—*Ernesto Sabato*

Everyone knows the story of Newton's apple. The theory of gravity is today the most basic scientific principle. However, in Newton's day the idea of gravity as a fundamental force in the universe was a very strange one. In fact, to most people back then, invisible forces acting on things from a distance was either demonic or divine.

Newton himself had a difficult time accepting the reality of "action at a distance." In fact he discouraged people from trying to figure out the true cause of gravity and to instead focus on the fact that his math and his experiments worked.

Using the lens of our contemporary time management culture, sitting in your garden in a "contemplative mood" is a complete waste of time. This (lack of) activity might indicate to some HR person that Newton was not necessarily a reliable employee. Did Newton have to add "5 pm: sit in garden, contemplate falling objects" to his to-do list? Does any reasonable person think that Sir Isaac Newton had a to-do list?

Newton was in fact known for his obsessive work ethic. He could sit in his garden and do nothing because it would never have occurred to Newton that sitting in his garden contemplating was the same thing as wasting time.

Today we find popular magazines telling us we need to schedule "downtime" because the demands of corporate-controlled schedules are inhuman. Of course people are not explicit about the root of the problem, and we are advised to "schedule" the time off as long as it doesn't conflict with our obligations. Downtime is actually advised as a way to optimize your productivity.

In the most literal sense, Newton was his own boss. He worked when he wanted to work, and he sat in his garden when it suited him. Naturally you will point out that this is impractical and unrealistic in the current economy. And I would say that we therefore deserve the paucity of intellectual dynamism that our economy compels.

Natural science before Newton was in a transformative phase. The period between the late 15th and 18th centuries is what many see as the crucial scientific revolution in human history. During time Copernicus, Kepler, Galileo, Brahe, and Newton each made enormous contributions to the advancement of the sciences. The 17th century especially saw an intellectual explosion that suddenly and massively increased our comprehension of the universe. Our knowledge about the natural world began expanding at an ever-accelerating rate that continues to this day. Human understanding of nature went from superstitious folk-belief to real science.

It was during this revolution that a scientific community came into being that published journals and started having meetings much like today's scientific conferences. In the centuries since Newton, natural science has met with astonishing success. Typically we think of Newton seeing the apple fall as some kind of serendipitous moment in the history of science. Whatever the origin of the story really is, after seeing the apple fall and after working out his theory Newton wrote one of the most significant scientific publications in history: the *Philosophiae naturalis principia mathematica*, in which the formal theory of gravity is introduced.

Newton wasn't holed up in his study tearing his hair out trying to figure out why objects move toward earth and the planets orbit the Sun, stressing about a looming deadline. Nor was a productivity expert looking over Newton's shoulder to make sure he was working efficiently. We can imagine that as he relaxed on a warm evening in his garden, the soothing noises of birds singing and leaves blowing in the breeze surrounding him, he either closed his eyes or looked at nothing in particular.

He would have had a feeling of well-being and sensations of positive emotions might have washed over him. All this would put him in a nice "contemplative mood." His default mode network would have started to increase its activity. Blood would have started flowing to his precuneous, his lateral parietal cortex, his medial prefrontal cortex, and his anterior cingulate cortex as these regions began to consume oxygen and glucose at an increased rate.

This is the default mode network getting warmed up. The neurons in these regions are increasing their activity. His anterior cingulate would have signaled to his parasympathetic nervous system that all was well and his blood pressure would drop. His heart rate would slow and time between beats would start to become slightly more variable.

This physiological reaction would start to feed back to his brain and his relaxation might deepen. In this idle state and in the absence of some externally induced task, Newton's brain starts to get to work. His mind begins to wander; his thoughts turn inward and become reflective.

The nodes in his default mode network are now ready to communicate. The millions of neurons in these regions begin to partially synchronize their oscillatory electrical activity at different frequencies so that neuronal messages from the default mode network can travel throughout his brain. Since the nodes in the default mode network are hubs they can get information from almost any brain region. Memories and associations, along with mathematical and spatial concepts, which are stored in regions connected to the parietal cortex, can also be accessed by his default mode network. These concepts now begin to bubble up into Newton's consciousness as the medial prefrontal cortex reports to the rest of the active default network what is happening in the far reaches of his subconscious.

These reports from Newton's vast knowledge of physics in his long-term memory, which are normally not part of his conscious awareness, can now enter his mind because his brain does not have to worry about talking, scheduling meetings, planning his day, or managing his time.

The motions of the planets, the inverse square law, attraction, mass, and acceleration: all of these concepts that Newton has learned might have begun circulating in Newton's awareness. Prior to sitting in his garden this particular evening, Newton might not have found relationships among these concepts because they would not have the chance to enter his awareness during his everyday life. Likewise, there is also evidence that the default mode network works unconsciously so that in an idle state, the brain finds connections among concepts without awareness.

Then for reasons we do not yet understand, sometimes these thoughts reach awareness. The important thing is that during rest, the default mode network can open connections between brain regions that are normally too busy trying to keep up with your activity-filled life to talk to each other. This is when true creativity and insight can happen. At this point, Newton's anterior cingulate cortex, normally hard at work detecting errors and monitoring the outcome of behavior, is now freed to detect weak and strange relationships between numbers, forces, objects, and space.

In such a relaxed state, Newton might have only barely noticed the apple falling from the tree. However, his brain would have recorded the event. A seemingly trivial event in the world, an apple falling from a tree, might have triggered a cascade of neural activity which allowed the concepts Newton was contemplating to synthesize into a completely new idea. All the clocks struck at the same time because the clocks were not being wound.

In fact, Newtonian mechanics is still used as the basis for modern engineering. Bridges, buildings, airplanes, and cars still rely on engineers being able to calculate using Newton's laws. A "Newton" is an indispensible unit of measurement that tells you how much force you need to move a mass of one kilogram at a rate of one meter per second squared.

Sitting around in contemplative moods is not exactly tolerated in the modern school or workplace. We have to wonder how many young potential Isaac Newton's we are stifling just so we can control them in school and at home. How much does the need to have focused and organized children arise from our obsessively organized adult lives? And why do our adult lives need to be obsessively organized?

We categorize adults who sit in contemplative moods as flakey, spacey, or lazy. But for your brain to do its best work, you need to be idle. If you want to have great ideas or if you just want to get know yourself, you must stop managing your time. At the very least, modern neuroscience is rapidly amassing more and more evidence that the resting state of the brain is vital to its health.

4

RILKE AND THE IDLE
EXAMINED LIFE

"The only journey is the one within."

—*Rainer M. Rilke*

Rilke was a sensitive person ill-suited to his times. The years following the turn of the 20th century in Europe saw the brutal birth of the modern industrial economy and the horrors of World War I. This period also saw the increasing obsession on the part of the capitalist class with measuring time and maximizing worker efficiency. And there are the first hints of the nascent time management industry beginning to wrap its tentacles around the culture. Clocks in offices, factories, and homes were becoming widespread for the first time. Human workers began to be thought of as machines in a system designed to produce profit for the owners of the economy. Against this backdrop, the sensitive and introspective Rilke sacrificed romantic love, his family, and material comforts in order to pursue his art.

Rilke knew that spending time doing nothing was extremely important for his creative process. He aspired to be idle with joy—which to our over-worked and over-scheduled 21st-century ears sounds shocking. Enjoying idleness is anathema to our cultural belief that without unrelenting activity we are somehow not living up to our potential, a belief which we are taught implicitly from infancy.

Modern neuroscience may show us that in fact the opposite is true—our true potential can only be realized through periods of doing nothing. As Oscar Wilde writes in the *Soul of Man Under Socialism*: "Humanity amusing itself, or enjoying cultivated leisure—which, and not labor, is the aim of man—or making beautiful things, or reading beautiful things, or simply contemplating the world with admiration and delight."

Recent research is revealing that some forms of self-knowledge may only appear to us in idle states. The default mode network activates not only when we are at rest, but also when we turn our attention to ourselves and *"spect intro."* Our mind begins to wander and the contents of our unconsciousness can percolate up into awareness. The default mode network allows us to process information that is related to social relationships, our place in the wider world, fantasies we have about the future, and of course: emotions.

Rilke spent much of his adult life actually wandering Europe in search of the ideal place—both physically and spiritually—in which to write poetry. He traveled to Russia and met Tolstoy, he spent time in Sweden, Italy, France, and finally ended up in Switzerland. His work was so important to some patrons that these wealthy people often paid for Rilke to live at their villas or castles while he worked—or, rather, did not work.

In fact, Rilke waited fifteen years between major volumes of poetry—from *New Poems* published in 1907 to what many consider his life's crowning achievements: *The Duino Elegies* and *Sonnets to Orpheus*, both in 1922. He wrote some poetry during those years; however he considered these "occasional" poems. *The Elegies* took over ten years to complete. Rilke's great poems came to him suddenly, and he regarded them as gifts from outside himself, perhaps from angels. Rilke described the experience of writing a poem as simply having to take dictation. One of his great translators, the American poet Robert Bly, writes how Rilke would occasionally miss a rhyme when trying to capture a poem because he could not write fast enough.

From a neuroscience perspective, Rilke was learning to let brain regions like the medial prefrontal cortex report images and associations from brain regions like the hippocampus and neocortex, whose deepest contents do not always enter awareness. In our constant struggle to achieve success or even just keep our jobs, we use the parts of our brain that process immediate external events. This externally focused network toggles off the default mode network and prevents us from accessing what may be going on in the rest of our brains. Yet our brains are perpetually generating and responding to emotions— and all this emotional energy must be dissipated somewhere.

Rilke also struggled with bouts of depression, possibly because he did not spare himself in his relentless self-examination. He allowed every ugly side of his internal world to surface to his consciousness so that he could scrutinize it. And here we can see the razor thin line between the peak of genius and the abyss of depression and madness: Rilke lived much of his whole adult life very close to that line.

"The lazy man does not stand in the way of progress. When he sees progress roaring down upon him he steps nimbly out of the way."
—*Christopher Morley, "On Laziness"*

Rilke's amazing ability to explore his unconscious and dredge up perhaps long forgotten scenes and emotions from his youth was likely the result of his brain's default mode network being allowed to be active while he was being idle.

For many people this can be a horrifying experience. There is probably a lot of stuff in your unconsciousness that you'd much rather leave there. Could it be that these uncomfortable things you are suppressing by scheduling your day to oblivion are knocking on the door to your consciousness for a reason? The common sense notion about "workaholics" is that they find idleness and inactivity to be unbearable because they are escaping emotional pain through constant work.

When children enter school, and increasingly even before they enter school, parents fill up their lives with a stream of activities: sports, early exposure music classes, Chinese immersion school, summer camps, volunteer soup kitchen duties, dressage lessons, theater coaching, mathletics, and science workshops. There seems to be a pervasive and deep-seated anxiety among a certain class of parents that their children might actually have time to hang around and be children.

Parents are forced to work longer and longer hours, sometimes just to keep the same pay. To replace ourselves we force our children to endure an endless barrage of activities that serve as proxy parents. We do this in order to convince ourselves that we still participate in some meaningful way in our children's lives.

We can get reports from teachers or coaches on our child's successes—all without actually ever seeing the child do the activity we signed them up for. After all, we have more important things to do, like work! It should come as no surprise that as "play dates" overtake simply hanging around with friends and actually playing outside, childhood anxiety and depression rates are soaring, in tandem with childhood obesity.

The current generation of children may be the first ever to have shorter life-expectancy than the previous generation. Whatever mountains of epidemiological and clinical evidence you need to convince yourself that this is real, the underlying cause is quite straightforward: children who do not spend several hours *every day* outside running around, hanging out with friends, not doing anything in particular, and instead spend every moment of every day doing parent-induced tasks and lessons, seeing friends on a schedule, eating massively processed food, and playing video games in order to virtually explore their worlds, become fat and depressed.

There are hundreds of books and magazine articles on time management for children with titles like *Organization; Time Management & Study Skills for Children*; *Late, Lost and Unprepared: A Parents' Guide to Helping Children with Executive Functioning*, and *Get That Kid Organized!*

For those achievement-obsessed parents and students for whom unnecessary pharmacological manipulation with amphetamine-derived ADHD medication is not financially or morally problematic, there are apparently plenty of academic-doping doctors who will prescribe ADHD medicine to undiagnosed students so they can attain artificial laser-like focus and crush their competition on the SATs.

These doctors are no different ethically from the shady underworld-doping doctors one finds in professional sports. And I would argue it is the same "win-at-all-costs" culture that breeds the desire to use any means necessary to attain what are essentially meaningless test results.

Forcing a child to become a pharmaceutically-enhanced and hyper-organized mini-adult at an early age removes the child's sense of control over her world. Depression and anxiety are highly correlated with people's sense of control over their own lives.

Psychologists have long used a questionnaire to assess the degree to which people feel control over their lives called the Rotter Internal-External Locus of Control Scale. If you score toward the internal end of the scale you feel that you are source of control over your life, and if you score toward the external end of the scale you feel that your life is controlled by someone or something other than you.

Several studies have shown that the more toward the internal end of the scale you are, the less likely you are to become depressed and anxious. When researchers analyzed data from the Rotter scale over a forty-two year period from 1960 to 2002, they found that scores have shifted from the internal end of the scale to the external. These scores had shifted so much that an average young person in 2002 was more external (felt that external forces controlled her life) than eighty percent of young people in the 1960s.

In 2010, *Newsweek* magazine ran a story devoted to what it called "The Creativity Crisis," which received moderate attention. *Newsweek* reported that scores on psychological tests that are designed to assess a child's creativity have been steadily declining since 1990.

This, despite the fact that IQs have been rising. After analyzing the data from around three hundred thousand children and adults, Kyng Hee Kim, a researcher at William & Mary, found that this decline in creativity is most pronounced in exactly the age group from which you'd expect the most creativity, kindergarten through sixth grade. As children become more scheduled, more measured, more managed to achieve, and more hijacked by digital media, they become less and less creative.

Rilke described entering school as entering captivity. Modern parents have become preoccupied with developmental activities that supposedly enhance their children's chances of success even before school begins, success as defined by grades, future salaries, and awards.

In Rilke's poem "Imaginary Biography," he describes the horror of starting school, which for me involved sobbing as my mother left me standing in the line of other seemingly happy kids at the kindergarten door:

First childhood, no limits, no renunciations, no goals.
Such unthinking joy.
Then abruptly terror, schoolrooms, boundaries, captivity,
and a plunge into temptation and deep loss.

Ironically for a culture obsessed with optimizing child development, increasing evidence about the brain shows that not having externally directed goals is crucial for the brain's development.

Through the constant external demands and activities in which they are forced to partake, plus countless hours spent using digital devices, children have less and less time to introspect, process social and emotional experiences, and self-reflect.

What's more, children may develop an uncomfortable relationship with their idle selves, like many adults. When this happens, becoming idle will initially induce a feeling very similar to what a smoker craving a cigarette experiences: restless desperation. The child will seek out external stimulation in digital devices, approval from teachers, or from other adults.

In a recent paper called "Rest is Not Idleness: Implications of the Brain's Default Mode for Human Development and Education," psychologists Mary Helen Immordino-Yang, Joanna Christodoulu, and Vanessa Singh hypothesize that allowing children to engage in free-form daydreaming and other types of inattentive states is essential to the development of social skills.

They review the last decade of evidence about the default mode network and discuss its implications for human development early in life and education. If the child's life is filled with "systematically high environmental attention demands," they posit that the process of developing the ability to reflect, create meaning from experience, and reconcile memories with current experience will be disrupted. A child's brain needs time to sift through everything that happens in a given day, consolidate these experiences, and integrate them into the larger self which is being formed through childhood.

The only way to allow this process to happen is to be idle. Turning off the outside world for a significant amount of time each day without demands or expectations is necessary for children. It could turn out that most of childhood should be free-form daydreaming, playing without purpose, and the experience of unthinking joy in order for later mental health.

In one of his *Letters to a Young Poet*, Rilke writes, "The quieter we are, the more patient and open we are in our sadnesses, the more deeply and unerringly a new revelation can enter us, and the more we can make it our own. Later on when it 'happens'—when it manifests in our response to another person—we will feel it as belonging to our innermost being."

Immordino-Yang et al. write that time and skills for what they call "constructive internal reflection" are beneficial for emotional learning and well-being. And when a child spends all day directing her attention to the external world her ability to understand "what this means for the world and the way I live my life" will be undermined.

Just as muscles need time to recover after exercise, our brains need time to recover after engagement with the external world. For example, research indicates that young people who send text messages extremely often tend to score lower on tests that measure moral reflectivity. This could be because with each new text, the task positive network is engaged, thereby suppressing activity in the default mode network. We start to identify more with the phone in our pockets than the mind in our heads.

Ostensibly, the long-term goal of Overachievement Oriented Parenting is to get one's child into a top university.[*] This is one of the most important symbolic displays of prestige we have in the United States. Once there, students experience a world of insane activity and busyness the likes of which they have never known. In a recent *Harvard Magazine* article by Craig Lambert about the university's "superhero undergraduates" a student says, "College here is like daring yourself to swim the length of a swimming pool without breathing. A lap is a semester. I want to do everything I possibly can." Naturally, she is completely exhausted. Her fatigue has several levels, first a "goofy feeling, like feeling drunk all the time; you're not quite sure what's going on." Next, she says "there's this extra level of exhaustion, where you feel dead behind your eyes. The last four weeks, that's where I've been. I get sick a lot." Getting sick a lot is seen as a sign that you are truly pushing yourself to your absolute limits. If you're not getting sick a lot, you're not trying hard enough.

Another student at Harvard quoted in the article marvels at how few intellectual discussions occur outside class. Apparently, if there is no officially-recognized academic advantage to be

---

[*] Not to be confused with Object Oriented Programming, also abbreviated as OOP.

gained by having an intellectual discussion, then it's pointless. Pursuing your own interests is even called "independent study" so that you can still write it on your CV, but students who actually have interests outside of padding their resumes are quite rare. Students are worried about having to "explain away" gaps on their resumes.

The majority of these students, it seems, have no idea what idleness is, much less how to enjoy it. They cannot see the intrinsic value of sitting at a café for several hours with a few friends discussing French cinema. Ironically, many of the people they are studying at Harvard were masters of idleness.

Jean-Paul Sartre and Simone de Beauvoir spent hours sitting at cafés debating each other or anyone who cared to join them. These intense discussions often served as the starting point for some of the couple's great work. Yet for this group of students with perfect academic credentials and thousands of hours of meticulously planned extracurricular activities, their time has been structured with purposeful tasks since they were toddlers.

The current generation of college undergrads at elite universities have been groomed, managed, coached, and steered without ever being allowed time to reflect on their true interests. According to the article, when Harvard does not schedule enough social activities, the students *and their parents* get anxious.

This kind of crazed and constant activity suppresses brain activity in the most important neural networks. We know too that depression and anxiety are associated with abnormalities in the default mode network. While there is no grand study linking all of these issues together, I believe a very strong case can be made that the way in which we are raising our kids—to be hyper-competitive overachievers—will in the long run increase their risk of mental and physical illness.

Overachievement Oriented Parenting is already making our children less creative, less social, and potentially less moral. Idleness, especially during childhood, could turn out to be critical to our development into moral and social beings. What can we learn from Rilke and Newton, two towering figures of science and literature? Both men sacrificed personal relationships and often their own well-being in order to pursue some higher intellectual purpose. In Newton's case his purpose was transforming math and science in ways which still affect our lives some three centuries later. Naturally, Isaac Newton possessed unique gifts which allowed him to see relationships among physical and mathematical concepts that few people in his day (or even today) could comprehend. Rilke's purpose was to dive as deep as he possibly could into his unconscious and discover universal truths about humanity.

In our hysterical rush to make money, gain status, compete for scarce jobs, jockey for promotions, make our kids athletic and intellectual geniuses, and organize our lives down to the second, we are suppressing our brain's natural ability to make meaning out of experience. It is through our brain's amazing natural meaning-making ability that real and profound creativity can happen. It is becoming clear that the resting state of the brain is essential to this process.

Had either Rilke or Newton lived today, their contributions to science and art may have been seriously compromised by the pressure to be productive.

5

YOU ARE A
SELF-ORGANIZING SYSTEM

"Self-organization: the appearance of structure or order without an external agent imposing it."

—*Francis Heylighen*

"… I soon understood that in serious work commanding and discipline are of little avail."

—*Peter Kropotkin*

The idea of self-organization goes against our mechanistic intuition about causation. Common sense says: things that are organized must have been made that way by some external intelligent force because order cannot just spontaneously appear. But this isn't true.

In nature, adaptive self-organization is the rule rather than the exception. Science and engineering have discovered that it is very difficult, if not impossible, to control self-organizing systems. Science has made valiant attempts at controlling events such as the weather, epileptic seizures, or spontaneous social movements. But these attempts have been in vain.

We can describe and predict weather, the brain, and social systems quite well. But we still can't explain them. Why has it proven so difficult for rulers, bosses, managers, dictators, capitalists, and time management gurus throughout history to control the most advanced self-organizing systems in the world?

Many scientists theorize that our economy is a self-organizing system. However, we will see that when these systems are pushed too far away from a state of what's called "criticality," they can collapse or completely change how they respond to the environment.

Whether the system we're talking about is an individual human being, an entire society, or the climate, staying within certain limits is essential for the system's stability. For humans, this might be why being idle is so important: it allows your system to return to what are called "stable dynamics."

According to the Polish physicists Jaroslaw Kwapien and Stanislaw Drozdz, a complex self-organizing system is "built from a large number of nonlinearly interacting constituents, which exhibits collective behavior and, due to an exchange of energy or information with the environment, can easily modify its internal structure and patterns of activity." Examples of these types of system are convective air masses, turbulence, fractal coastlines—and of course, brains.

Unfortunately, there is a trend in the organizational leadership literature to use complexity science for the goal of business success. The strange thing is that no one is suggesting yet that we should instead use the brain's self-organized behavior as a model to argue against imposing external organization on your life, since this more accurately reflects the brain's composition and dynamics.

Self-organization is a feature of complexity. It sometimes goes by another name: emergence. This means that complex behavior of a system displays macroscopic characteristics that none of the system's constituent parts display.

Extremely complex behavior at the system level can emerge from the interaction of simpler parts of the system. One illustrative and intuitive example is an ant colony. E.O. Wilson's book *The Superorganism* describes the amazing societies that ants and other social insects build. These insect societies are called "superorganisms" because even though they are made up of thousands or even millions of individual ants, ant colonies adapt and behave as if they are one being.

Ants are among the most successful species on the planet. The number of ants alive at any given time has been estimated to be around ten million billion. And given that a human weighs approximately one to two million times as much as an ant, ants and humans have roughly the same global biomass.

Ant colonies are capable of very complicated behavior. For instance, ant colonies can learn. A colony quickly finds the best route to a food source, the best place to dispose of dead ants, and even learns to regulate the internal temperature of a nest. Yet each ant has a very tiny brain. An individual ant has no idea what it is doing. How does the extremely organized complex behavior of ant colonies arise out of millions of dumb ants each doing their own thing? Especially given that an ant colony has no command and control structure.

An individual ant follows a set of very simple rules when going about its daily business, based on whether he's a worker, a drone, or a soldier. These behavioral algorithms appear to be genetically inherited. For example, ants follow a simple rule when meeting a moving object and sweeping their antennae over it: if the object smells like I do, I follow it. If the object doesn't smell like me, I will kill it. Sometimes, ants do this to the point where they follow each other to their doom, in what is known as an "ant death spiral."

Ants also spread information through chemical trails. When following other ants, they can smell the trails and know to turn left or right. Forager ants that find food sources begin leaving a certain chemical trail, and telling other ants to follow them. Soon a column of ants is headed toward the food.

Thus information about the location of a food source spreads quickly through the colony. An individual ant follows several of these simple rules using its sensory organs. When millions of these ants interact the self-organized complexity of the colony emerges. For instance, many individual ants will become suicidal in defense of the greater colony. Adaptive knowledge and information can be processed by the colony, but not by individual ants. Therefore, there are certain attributes of the colony that no individual ant has.

Consider a football team: the team has properties that each player does not, one of which is being a football team made of eleven players. Certain behaviors are only visible at the colony level of description. Yet if we examine each ant, we find a rather simple creature capable of only making quick decisions. While each ant is programmed to do a limited number of things based on context (find and carry food, follow or attack other ants), an ant colony can learn the best route to a food source, can build enormous networks of tunnels and nests, and can even grow fungus in complicated underground gardens.

Both ant colonies and brains are examples of spontaneously occurring macroscopic order from a vast ocean of randomly interacting parts on a microscopic level. When you have millions of simple ants obeying just a few rules, the possible outcomes of these ants interacting can become enormous.

In fact just one "computer" ant following only two simple rules seems to behave like a complex dynamical system. In computer science, there is a famous cellular automata model called Langton's ant. Imagine an ant called Langton randomly walking around on a grid made of black or white squares. Langton only has two rules: (1) when he lands on a white square he turns 90 degrees to the right, flips the color of the square to black and moves forward one square, (2) when he lands on a black square he turns 90 degrees to the left, flips the square to white and moves forward one unit. No matter how you set up the grid initially, no matter what arrangement of black and white squares you use as an initial configuration, after about ten thousand steps, Langton will start making a repetitive "highway" pattern of one hundred and four steps for infinity.

In other words, no matter how he starts off, Langton will converge on this complex pattern. This is only one ant, using only two rules. Langton provides insight as to how the behavior of ant colonies can be so spectacular in the real world. An example of self-organized ant colony behavior that is particularly intriguing comes from colonies of New World tropical army ants.

When the colony is resting during the day (even ants are idle!), it would be a waste of time to build labor-intensive nests. Instead, the ants form a shelter called a bivouac using their own massed bodies to protect the queen and young ants from intruders. The ants connect their bodies to each other and form into a kind of tent structure all without a boss ant telling them what to do.

The temperature and humidity inside the shelter is tightly regulated by the ants adjusting the shape and position of the bivouac. To forage for food, a column of hundreds of thousands of ants streams out of the shelter, grabs anything that moves, and reverses direction back into the colony, behaving like one organism stretching out an arm. During the night, the shelter dissipates and the colony moves onto the next site.

It is important to realize that each ant cannot have any idea that he is forming a part of the overall bivouac structure; much less that he is a member of a larger colony. To the individual ant, he is just connecting to his neighbors because the time of day, the temperature, or other environmental cues have exceeded a threshold that triggers his "connect to my neighbor's body" rule.

Similarly, the individual neurons in our brains do not in themselves know that they are part of your brain, or that they make up "you." Your consciousness is very much like the army ant's bivouac. One of the persistent philosophical illusions we've had for centuries is that there is some place in our brain where a little person named Homunculus controls the actions of our brains. Or that even without Homunculus, there is a specific part of the brain that is somehow the command and control center, dictating what the brain should do.

What neuroscience has revealed is that there is no such control center in the brain. There are hubs in our brain networks whose activity is more influential than others; however, there is no one single hub that dictates action. Our brains are much more like an ant colony: billions of neurons collaborating to give rise to our selves without any external or internal agent. In other words you are an emergent self-organizing phenomenon.

Neurons, like ants, follow algorithms and make quick binary decisions based on signals they receive. When a certain electrochemical threshold has been reached by incoming signals to a neuron, and its oscillation is in partial synchrony with its neighbors, it fires an action potential which propagates to other neurons to which it is connected. This activity can cause other neurons downstream either to fire or not to fire depending on the context. The appearance of extremely complex organization arises from the interaction of billions of smaller and simpler parts.

The interaction of billions of individual neurons using trillions of connections allows for the emergence of the infinite array of human creativity, just as an ant colony is much more creative and adaptive than an individual ant. Naturally, the comparison between ants and humans only goes so far. And as I've pointed out, the analogy really only works at the level of neurons in the brain. An individual human cannot be equated with a worker, a drone, or a soldier ant. The number of behavioral rules an individual human follows is not known, and is potentially infinite.

We can also become aware of what rules we are following and exercise a degree of choice over them. And most importantly, humans can create novel rules to follow. Yet there is one important aspect in which our brains and ant colonies are very similar: as complex self-organizing systems they have adapted to certain parameters. When these parameters are pushed too far, for example by climate change, ant colonies can collapse.

Because individual ants have very few degrees of freedom in their behavior, their collective behavior is very harmonious with the environment. It's the same with the individual neurons in our brains; they live harmoniously together in our skulls. In contrast to an ant, a human brain as a whole has a potentially unlimited number of degrees of freedom. This gives us our unique intelligence and creativity. It may be what also prevents us from enjoying slavery—unlike an individual ant.

Bertrand Russell defined work as, first, altering the position of matter at or near the earth's surface relatively to other such matter; second, telling other people to do so. He goes on to say that the first is unpleasant and ill-paid; the second is pleasant and highly paid.

6

REVOLUTION OR SUICIDE

"This is why Foxconn workers are free to jump from buildings but not to 'make trouble.'"

—Foxconn worker

"Specialization is for insects."
—Bart Kosko, professor, USC; author of Noise

Soviet farm collectivization in the 1930s and the agricultural development of the American colonies were attempts to impose structure onto groups of humans from the top down for the benefit of those in power. A small cadre of powerful people in each society desired either symbolic or economic power, and so they implemented a system of authoritarian order on the society in order to achieve their goals.

People did not willingly participate in these projects—they had to be threatened with severe punishments and constantly monitored to make sure they kept working.

Nature frequently resists being managed. "Scientific forestry," for instance, was invented in the 18th century in Germany as an attempt to gain control over the unruly natural forests. State bureaucrats desired more yields from certain trees, which they could not reliably get from old growth forests. And they needed to precisely measure and quantify the output of the forest.

Anthropologist James C. Scott describes the rise of scientific forestry in his influential book *Seeing Like a State.* The scientific foresters replaced the complex ecosystems in the natural forests with simplified "scientific" forests for maximizing yields of certain types of timber. They planted the forests to resemble an Excel spreadsheet: row upon row of neatly-ordered trees all of the same type. A monoculture. In the first generation, this all worked marvelously well: yields were up, the timber was easy to harvest, and the bureaucrats could efficiently count the trees in order to make predictions about the future.

Inevitably, the forests revolted. Within one generation, yields for some trees were down thirty percent. The perplexed Germans invented a word for what happened: *Waldsterben* (forest death). This was when the nutrient cycle of the soil was altered beyond the point of repair by the monoculture trees. In the worst cases, the entire forest died. The reason "scientific forestry" failed was due to total scientific ignorance of how forests work.

Forests, too, are self-organizing systems. Their health is maintained by an extremely complex interaction between diverse types of soil, animals, insects (such as ants), plants, fungus, trees, and weather. By disrupting this exquisitely balanced and harmonious system through uniformity and attempting to make the forest "productive," scientific forestry caused the forest ecosystem to collapse. Surely the principles of "scientific forestry" were consigned to history's ash heap? Consider Apple. Surely Apple, the most valuable company in the world, the maker of the coolest digital devices known to humanity, eschews the antiquated principles of German scientific forestry?

You have likely heard of the abysmal working conditions at the Chinese factories that produce nearly all our electronics. Your passing concern might have been assuaged by the recent announcements that the factories are attempting to make work at these places more worker-friendly. Apple's products are manufactured by a Taiwanese company in China called Foxconn. Foxconn proudly employs what are called "scientific management" techniques for its millions of workers.

The rationale for doing this is always the same: a small group of powerful people wish to control systems that are intrinsically uncontrollable so that these systems can be made to do things they would not otherwise do. These short-term solutions are always greeted as a revelation. They certainly produce stellar short term results.

But whether we are talking about forests or human beings, the scientific fact about these systems is that they are self-organized, and therefore an external agent cannot control them. Forcing them to suppress their natural fluctuations and complexities in the name of productivity will always lead to revolution, crisis, or collapse. In the case of forests, you get *Waldsterben*. For human beings, you may get suicide. You may get the collapse of a corporation or an entire manufacturing sector.

Foxconn's approach to management is quite simple: make each human do a very specialized repetitive task so that no actual thought or skill is required. This type of specialized labor works in ant colonies because individual ants are relatively simple creatures and are by genetic design already specialized to do certain tasks without thinking.

Human beings are actually terrible at specialization. This is why every attempt to turn human beings into worker insects for the benefit of rich people results in massive human misery. Terry Gou, the CEO of Foxconn, admits as much in one of his sayings that people who wish to get promoted must memorize: "Suffering is the identical twin of growth."

In a remarkable study by Pun Ngai and Jenny Chan about the rash of recent suicides at the Apple supplier, they describe the fate of seventeen-year-old worker Tian Wu who on March 17, 2010 jumped from the fourth floor of her worker dormitory.[5] Tian had just moved to Longchua to work at the Foxconn factory from rural Hubai. Prior to what she called "her accident" she was described as a carefree girl who loved flowers.

---

[5] The study, "Global Capital, the State, and Chinese Workers: The Foxconn Experience" details the horrific conditions in which the workers who make Apple products must live and work. It reveals Apple's complicity in keeping wages low and worker rights to a minimum. Before you buy your next über-cool Apple product or read Walter Isaacson's gushing biography of Steve Jobs, I highly recommend reading this study, available for free online.

After working at the Foxconn Longhua campus for thirty-seven days she attempted suicide. Unlike fourteen of her co-workers who also attempted suicide during a two-month span in 2010 and 2011, Tian survived. She will likely be confined to a wheelchair for the rest of her life.

Foxconn maintains a round-the-clock production schedule and often imposes overtime on the workers. They live in dormitories that have armed security guards at the doors. They live in such close quarters that personal privacy is next to nonexistent. Workers are randomly assigned to dorm rooms, a process which breaks up existing social networks and keeps worker organization to a minimum. They are not allowed visitors overnight. The entire life of a Foxconn worker is devoted to the production of cheap electronics, mostly for Western consumption.

Recently, pressure has been mounting on Apple and other technology companies to examine their relationships to their Chinese suppliers like Foxconn. However, I would argue that it is the fundamental nature of the work that drives people to suicide. Working at Foxconn is the logical extreme of time management. Management schedules washing, eating, and sleeping to coincide with production timelines and in order to maximize the efficiency of shift rotation.

In the West, we are proud of our new economy based on mobility and of our information revolution. We seem to regard industrial production as a quaint relic of the mid-20th century, as if we're somehow now free of the ugliness and unhipness of manufacturing. We all live in the cloud now. In fact, Foxconn is the largest private employer in all China. It employs upwards of

1.4 million people, and one of the factory compounds employs four hundred thousand people. That's four hundred thousand people—roughly the population of Minneapolis—working at one factory.

The Fair Labor Association recently investigated Foxconn and concluded, "The factories were working beyond legal and code limits on hours of work, not recording and paying unscheduled overtime correctly, allowing interns to work overtime against Chinese regulations and during peak periods workers worked more than seven days in a row without a rest day. In addition the investigation recorded many health and safety issues and found that although there is a trade union with a collective bargaining agreement it does not measure up to international or national standards."

One Foxconn worker comments, "We get yelled at all the time. It's very tough around here. We're trapped in a 'concentration camp' of labor discipline—Foxconn manages us through the principle of 'obedience, obedience, and absolute obedience!' Must we sacrifice our dignity as people for production efficiency?" In this inhumane environment, Ngai's study found small acts of resistance among the workers such as stealing products, slow-downs, stoppages, small-scale strikes, and sometimes even sabotage, which really delays production.

Then there are of course the suicides, the final option for workers to exert control over their lives. The system—in this case, the worker's brain—tries to inject variation into its life—the stealing and sabotage—to find a more stable space in which the intrinsic dynamics of the system are in balance with the environment.

Complex systems exist very close to the edge between order and disorder—this is called "self-organized criticality," and it allows these systems to adapt to new environments. At this edge of chaos, systems rapidly change their internal structures until they find a stable state. There are limits to this adaptability however, and they are nonlinear. They can reach a threshold beyond which the system completely and catastrophically falls apart. A striking example of this is how glaciers melt. They can withstand a certain amount of warming, but when the melting has reached a certain threshold (the popular term for this is "tipping point") the glacier will start to disappear even if the temperature drops again.

Sand piles are often used to illustrate how self-organized systems stay on the edge of order and disorder, and to illustrate the concept of a nonlinear threshold. Imagine a completely flat surface on which you pour grains of sand at some constant rate. The grains of sand fall randomly to either side of the pile as it builds up. At first, the pile is small and so the angle of its slope is very shallow. You can keep adding sand and the pile will just get taller.

At a certain point, the angle of the pile will become steep enough so that adding more sand causes small avalanches. Eventually, the angle of the pile and the frequency of the avalanches will converge to form a balance so that the overall shape of the pile is maintained. However, the key to this is that there is an open dissipation of sand running off the pile to compensate for the new sand being poured on to the pile. If you keep adding sand, the pile angle will become so steep that when you add just one more grain of sand, it will cause a catastrophic avalanche that flattens the whole pile.

Working nonstop has become a new badge of honor among the professional digital class. We walk around with our gadgets trying to define our value propositions. The compulsion that businesses have to organize our lives with apps and calendars comes from deep ignorance of how the brain actually functions. We refuse to recognize that our brains are already a miracle of complex organization.

Albert Einstein, in a much-overlooked 1949 essay called "Why Socialism?", wrote, "If we ask ourselves how the structure of society and the cultural attitude of man should be changed in order to make human life as satisfying as possible, we should constantly be conscious of the fact that there are certain conditions which we are unable to modify. As mentioned before, the biological nature of man is, for all practical purposes, not subject to change."

While our understanding of "the biological nature of man" is constantly being updated, Einstein was correct in realizing that our brains have limits. Though our lives are easier, we exist on the same spectrum as a Chinese laborer. The price of achievement is the same price. Increasingly, information companies are trying to have "flat" organizations. However, the less explicit the hierarchy is at a job, the more responsibility each worker is typically expected to take. The line between life and work is blurred as the endless list of tasks becomes distributed to everyone.

Your mobile devices ensure you are available 24/7 to handle work-related requests. There is no longer any physical place in which you are not able to work. Your mind can never truly rest. A modern information worker may actually never feel she is not working. From the point of view of capitalist investors, inducing this fear of losing an endless competition is more effective than employing bosses to intimidate workers. This compulsion to work is a form of externally imposed order and it can be a schedule, a to-do list, a business process, inane projects, and time management activities, or directives from a customer who wanted results six months ago.

At the other end of the spectrum, we find workers like Tian Wu at the Foxconn factories in China. They pay the price of our digital mobility, sometimes with their lives. Anarchist Mikhail Bakunin wrote, "The freedom of all is essential to my freedom." What he meant was that if some of us are enslaved, none of us are truly free.

In *Wealth of Nations*, Adam Smith writes, "Great labour, either of mind or body, continued for several days together, is in most men naturally followed by a great desire of relaxation, which, if not restrained by force or by some strong necessity, is almost irresistible. It is the call of nature, which requires to be relieved by some indulgence, sometimes of ease only, but sometimes too of dissipation and diversion. If it is not complied with, the consequences are often dangerous, and sometimes fatal, and such as almost always, sooner or later, bring on the peculiar infirmity of the trade. If masters would listen to the dictates of reason and humanity, they have frequently occasion rather to moderate, than to animate the application of many of their workmen."

We must ask why, and for whom, are we doing all this work? Recall that your brain has hundred billion neurons, each connected by two hundred trillion synapses. Its activity is regulated by a spectacular orchestra of electrical activity that synchronizes and desynchronizes neurons and brain regions to produce the complex harmony that allows us to be human beings.

An underlying assumption of productivity and time management is that the natural way human beings work must be suppressed for the sake of organization and productivity. For instance, time management expert David Allen's productivity strategy is to remove non-essential thoughts from your brain. He admonishes us to get whatever we're stressing about out of our brains and into some type of preferably automated to-do list manager: such as one of the countless productivity apps on your iPhone. Errands, emails to write, bills to pay, accounts to manage, inventories to check, strategic marketing plans to syntheoptimergize, whatever occurs to you during the course of your hectic day. When you have a physical record of these tasks, they don't have to occupy memory space in your brain, you are less likely to forget them, and you don't have to worry about them.

Nowhere in Allen's imperative to "become a wizard of productivity" does he suggest that if you must rely on perpetual mnemonic and digital gymnastics to get through your day, maybe you have too much to do. As I've pointed out, the human brain has limits. A modern scientific understanding of our brains shows that each of us has a unique order and structure, which we must learn to understand as much through idleness as activity.

This uniqueness is also what unites us. Recognizing what is universal in humans—self-organization, complexity, and non-linearity—should liberate and relax us. Self-organizing dynamics are fundamental to how our brains process information. Our nervous system is also a nonlinear dynamic system coupled to our brain. It is our heart's ability to flexibly respond to changes in activity that prevents stroke or heart attack. Reduced heart rate variability is a very good predictor of poor cardiac health.

And it turns out that parts of the brain's default mode network are tightly coupled to regulating variable cardiac rhythms. The anterior cingulate cortex, among other regions, plays an important role in regulating the stress that gets transferred to our heart. Idleness lets the ACC and our nervous system find stable and variable dynamics. Stress reduces the variability in our heart rate: a low level of anxiety forces the heart to be in a state of preparedness, which it cannot maintain indefinitely.

An extreme example of disorder in this system is post-traumatic stress disorder (PTSD). People with PTSD feel like they are constantly on vigil; they can never relax for fear of something violent happening to them again. Therefore, their hearts are constantly on alert, which reduces the variability in its rhythm. Constant overwork can be thought of as a mild form of PTSD.

As Einstein indicated, we should each have the freedom to allow our own order and structure to emerge naturally and spend our days as we wish. Everyone hates working for other people. And being insanely busy all the time is not only bad for you; it also prevents you from discovering the human being you were meant to be.

7

THE SIGNAL IS THE NOISE

*"As he walked up and down ... he suddenly stopped dead—for he
seemed to hear a voice call through the roar of the wind."*

—*Donald Prater*, A Ringing Glass:
the Life of Rainer Maria Rilke

In 1912, Rilke was staying at an Italian castle called Duino, owned
by a Czech princess. Before coming to Duino, Rilke had been
struggling for quite some time. He was still trying to learn how
to listen to his unconscious for what he called his life's next "turn."

Rilke spent hours every day at the castle walking near the
two-hundred-foot cliffs which overlooked the rough sea. It had
been several years since he had written any significant poems.
One morning, he received an irritating and tedious business letter. Annoyed, he decided to take his walk on the path between two
giant concrete battlements of the castle, near the sheer drop to the
sea. A strong Adriatic wind was blowing, called a *bora* in Italian.

As Donald Prater describes, Rilke heard a voice call through
the roar of the wind. What the voice said to him became one of

the poet's most famous lines: *Wer, wenn ich schriee, hörte mich denn aus der Engel Ordnungen?*

> *And if I cried out, who would hear me up there among the angelic orders?*

Did Rilke hear the wind "speak" that day at the coastal castle? I suggest that the mechanism of "stochastic resonance" helped Rilke suddenly enter a state of heightened awareness.

Stochastic resonance describes any phenomenon where the presence of noise, either internally or externally, in a nonlinear system makes the system respond better than it would without noise. In nonlinear dynamical systems—like the brain—noise can make the system behave in a more orderly fashion. It can also boost weak internal or external signals so that our sensory organs and even our conscious awareness can detect them. Noise and stochastic resonance are essential to consciousness.

When Rilke stepped out onto to the path at the castle that morning, and into the roar of the wind, perhaps the noise amplified a weak signal from deep within Rilke's mind: *If I cried out, who would hear me?*

Rilke wrote this line down in a small notebook that he always had with him. He went back to his room, and by evening, the entire first elegy had been composed. He wrote furiously, trying to capture the torrent of words that were now flooding from his consciousness. It was as if the dam inside his brain had burst.

We almost always think of noise as bad. It is a form of interference. It is a nuisance. Too much of it over time can cause hearing loss. Electrical engineers have been struggling to get rid of noise in their systems since the invention of the telephone and computer. Jet engine manufacturers face severe restrictions nowadays on how loud their engines can be near airports. Commercial jetliners are about fifty percent quieter today than they were just twenty years ago.

Nate Silver, in his great book *The Signal and the Noise*, says of noise, "The signal is the truth. The noise is what distracts us from the truth." While Silver's characterization of the signal and the noise reflects our common sense intuition about noise, there are many circumstances in which the addition of the right amount of noise actually boosts the signal.

Given the ubiquity of noise in the brain and the environment, it is not surprising that evolution has endowed biological systems with the ability to use noise to find the signal. In fact if our brains were without randomness, they would not be able to function.

The great thing about our brains is that they have evolved to find signals and truth without any real effort on our part. In fact our brains do a better job of finding our own truth if we are idle.

In the noise field, stochastic resonance (abbreviated as SR) has become an important area of research over the last thirty years. Here's the revelation: in nonlinear systems, adding a certain optimal amount of noise actually increases the signal-to-noise ratio. In other words, adding noise to a faint signal might actually make the signal stronger.

An Italian physicist at the NATO International School of Climatology named Roberto Benzi introduced SR in the early 1980s to explain the recurrence of the Earth's ice-age cycle, which happens every one hundred thousand years. This is also the cycle of the eccentricity of the Earth's orbit. The idea very simply is that there are two "energy wells" or a double well that represent two states of the climate—frozen or warm—that the earth oscillates between.

When the Earth is in one side of the well it's on average much warmer; when it's on the other side of the well it's much colder on average. Benzi postulated that the combination of random or "stochastic" perturbations in the orbit in addition to the eccentricity was what caused the climate cycle; in other words, it was noise. He called the combination of eccentricity and noise "stochastic resonance" to mean that the noise amplified the effect of the eccentricity. In Earth's case, the source of the noise was small random wobbles in the eccentric orbit that pushed the state of the climate into one state or the other.

Consider the following diagrams:

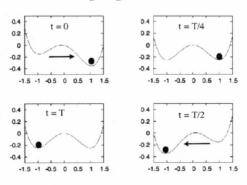

Imagine that the black marble in the picture represents the state of the climate at any given time.

The wavy line the marble is resting on represents the Earth's orbit. When the climate is in one of the wells (+1 or −1) it is either an ice-age or warm. When time (t) = 0 in the upper left illustrations, the probability that the climate will jump to the opposite state is very low.

Imagine now that we animate these illustrations and the wavy lines move up and down, and also start to jiggle around randomly. What makes the marble jump from one dip to the other?

The resonance happens when the noise and the orbit combine in just the right way to produce a large change and the marble jumps over the threshold, which could not happen without the noise.

One of the most famous demonstrations in biology of SR came in the 1990s when a group led by Frank Moss at the University of Missouri at St. Louis showed that paddlefish use electrical noise in muddy river water to locate their prey.

Paddlefish feed on plankton in North American rivers. The turbulence and mud make for conditions of near zero visibility. And plankton are tiny. The "paddle" on the paddlefish is actually an electrosensory antenna that responds to the low frequency electrical fields that the plankton emit.

A giant group of plankton causes background noise in the water. Moss's group found that when they injected an optimal amount of electrical noise into water the paddlefish were able to find plankton that were farther away. This noise enhancement was also demonstrated in the mechano-receptors of crayfish, the antenna of crickets, and in the brains of rats.

Human and animal neurons are nonlinear threshold devices, and as such they actually experience benefits from noise. In fact, it is likely that without noise they would not function at all. When something excites a brain enough, it temporarily changes its dynamics completely. In the case of a neuron it goes from resting to firing off an action potential.

Our neurons communicate with each other via an unbelievably complicated choreography that involves the electrical and chemical coordination of firing patterns among these neurons. Signals travel back and forth, partially synchronizing or desynchronizing their activity as necessary. Each neuron has a dynamic threshold for firing action potentials. In other words, the thresholds change over time. Neurons respond randomly and differently to stimuli, and this response is then randomly integrated to the network to which the neuron belongs.

With around hundred billion neurons packed into your skull, each firing hundreds of times per second, the inside of the brain is filled with noise. But is this noise bad? It could be that the spontaneous, intrinsic activity of the default mode network provides the necessary background noise for the brain to be able to process information. Abnormal functioning of the default mode network might give you too much or too little brain noise.

Noise can in fact help neurons detect weak signals from the environment or from other neurons.

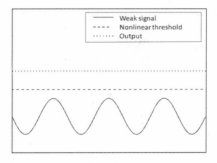

The figure above shows a typical sinusoidal wave represented by the blue line—aka "the signal." This could be anything from a sound, an image, a train of action potentials from other neurons, or perhaps even a great poem in your unconsciousness. The dotted line represents the neuron's threshold for firing.

Note that the blue line never crosses the threshold. Therefore, the solid black line above the dotted line that represents the output of the neuron does nothing. This is a weak signal without noise. It is undetectable.

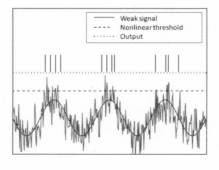

Now look what happens when we add the right level of noise to the blue signal, represented by the jagged and squiggly red line. Parts of the noise cross the neuron's threshold (dotted black line) and therefore the neuron fires action potentials, represented by the sold black vertical bars above the black output line.

Notice that where the noise crosses the threshold and causes the neurons to fire, the firing rate corresponds with the frequency of the underlying signal. Therefore the output characterizes the weak signal.

Information is actually transmitted by the noise.

This mechanism also works on the sensory level, so that noise amplifies sub-threshold sounds. Noise can also enhance weak images. A well-known image in the literature on the visual perception of stochastic resonance is Big Ben in London (reproduced from Simonotto, 1998).

On the left, Big Ben is digitized on a 1–256 gray scale at a 256 by 256 pixel resolution.

Each pixel in the picture fires when it crosses a threshold, using the same kind of algorithm as the brain's neurons.

Turning up the noise a little bit by increasing the maximum and minimum random values produces the middle image. This is the resonant noise intensity.

This noise level plus the signal—the weak image of Big Ben—creates the clear image in the middle. The right amount of noise improves the signal to noise ratio. Turning the noise up too high creates the degraded image on the right. When you plot this on a graph, you get what is called an inverted U shaped curve.

"Were you not always distracted by yearning, as though some lover were about to appear?"

—Rilke, from the first Duino Elegy

During graduate school in Sweden, I studied how noise might help children with Attention Deficit Hyperactivity Disorder, working together with psychologist Sverker Sikström. He developed a model of how stochastic resonance interacts with the dopamine system in the brain, based on the counterintuitive discovery by psychologist Göran Söderlund that ambient environmental noise actually helps children with ADHD remember a list of instructions. We theorized that noise could be a replacement for amphetamines.

People with ADHD often have very short working memory spans. "Working memory" refers to the ability to temporarily hold information in the brain once it disappears from the environment. Someone rattles off their phone number: how long can you remember the seven digits? Which digits do you remember, and for how long?

We rarely need to engage our working memories very often thanks to mobile technology. However, working memory turns out to be a central cognitive function. If you have poor working memory you're probably bad at a lot of other things: like time management.

Scientists think the working memory deficit in ADHD is related to dopamine function in the prefrontal cortex. Dopamine is one of a family of neurotransmitters that are synthesized by your brain. Without these neurotransmitters, you would not be able to think or to feel anything. This family includes serotonin, norepinephrine, and acetylcholine.

Dopamine underlies many important brain functions like learning, memory, pleasure, and motivation. ADHD children must be very highly motivated to do whatever requires their attention. The idea is that due to genetic mutations that lead to low levels of what is called tonic dopamine (the constant level of dopamine in your brain between your synapses), people with ADHD have an exaggerated "bursty" or phasic dopamine response to internal or external stimulation.

Because the brain is always trying to maintain homeostasis, some imbalance will often be addressed by a compensatory mechanism. In the case of low tonic dopamine, the ADHD brain compensates by releasing a very large phasic dopamine response to any signal.

This is a burst of dopamine, much like the one you get from doing something rewarding like smoking a cigarette, having whiskey, having sex, taking cocaine, drinking wine, eating very expensive chocolate, or of course doing nothing at all. This dopamine rush overwhelms the ADHD brain and it cannot help but focus on it.

For people struggling with ADHD, nearly anything in their environment can cause a huge burst of dopamine. Even more disconcerting, their own internal thoughts and impulses can sometimes cause these large releases of dopamine. In "normal" brains, the extra dopamine released into the spaces between your synapses by something rewarding is then sucked back up so that the balance between tonic and phasic dopamine can be maintained. But the tonic or constant level of dopamine remains high. This allows you to remain focused and motivated.

In an ADHD brain, too much dopamine is being sucked up so that there is very little dopamine in the inter-synaptic spaces and too much dopamine is being released in response to events. Therefore, children with ADHD are hypersensitive to environmental stimuli. This might explain many of the behaviors displayed by children with ADHD: distractibility, impulse control, trouble staying focused, and disorganization. They are constantly thrown between two extremes on a spectrum: cycling back and forth from extreme arousal to complete disinterest.

Amphetamines and cocaine block the reuptake of dopamine and cause more dopamine to be released. Small doses of amphetamine-derivative drugs calm people with ADHD and allow them to focus. Through blocking the excessive reuptake of dopamine in the ADHD brain, these drugs increase the tonic level of dopamine in the brain, while simultaneously reducing the intensity of phasic bursts of dopamine.

Cocaine is pleasurable because it not only blocks the reuptake of dopamine, but it also causes an even bigger flood of dopamine to be released. Over time, the brain stops synthesizing and releasing dopamine on its own because it adapts to having the artificial source.

Without dopamine, life is extremely uninteresting and unrewarding. We do not know at this point what the long-term effects of ADHD medication are, especially on healthy young brains. It is entirely possible that some form of adaption could occur, and less natural dopamine would be produced, which could lead to problems such as depression later in life.

We wondered whether ambient background noise would have a similar effect as amphetamine does for children with ADHD. The idea is that more noise in the environment would allow tonic dopamine in the ADHD brain to facilitate better memory performance. In other words, children with ADHD would require more environmental noise than children without ADHD in order to be able to concentrate.

When we had children with ADHD perform a visual memory task where they had to remember the locations of a sequence of squares on a grid after seeing them for only one second, they could typically only remember the locations of three or four squares. However, while listening to background noise they could remember five, six, or even seven locations, which is the typical visual-spatial working memory span for school-age children.

Using EEG, we saw a dramatic increase in the strength of brain's response while the ADHD children were listening to noise. The increased neural response could mean that ADHD brains need background noise to stimulate them into working just a little bit harder to perform the tasks of everyday life. The noise, like amphetamine, provides a better tonic level of dopamine that enables children to commit more sustained attention to task relevant information. I suspect that there is a strong cultural and economic component to the increasing rates of ADHD. As the demands of our economy increase in unhealthy ways, the proportion of children who in the past would not have been pushed to the ADHD end of the spectrum are finding themselves unable to cope.

While anywhere from two to ten percent of school age children have ADHD, up to forty percent of prison inmates have ADHD. Children with untreated ADHD have an increased risk for developing drug addiction in adulthood. Likely, these people who might have slipped through the many cracks in our educational and mental health care systems are self-medicating with substances and dosages that can easily hijack their brains.

Interestingly, children with ADHD also show decreased network integrity in their default mode network. It appears that one of the nodes of their default mode network, their precuneous, is not as well integrated into the network as it should be. In a resting state, the spontaneous fluctuations in the default mode networks of children with ADHD appear to oscillate faster than in "normal" children. In other words, these children are actually on a different wavelength. Children with ADHD have a hard time "switching off" their default mode networks. They must work to rest.

Just as noise in the Earth's orbit helps it to change between climate cycles on a thousand-year time scale, perhaps noise helps the ADHD brain toggle between task positive and task negative networks on a one-second time scale via the mechanism of stochastic resonance. If you have an MRI scanner, some EEG equipment, twenty or thirty children with ADHD, some crackerjack programmers, a free Saturday, a colossal amount of patience, some candy for the children, and some whiskey for the adults, you could probably do this experiment yourself. Let me know how it goes.

"Hence, it appears timely to turn [noise] from a nuisance into a virtue."
—*Thomas Wellens, noise physicist*

Even if you don't have ADHD, amphetamines improve your memory and concentration while you have elevated dopamine levels. Students have already discovered this, and abuse amphetamine derivative ADHD medication in order to power through ultramarathon study sessions.

We know that people with ADHD tend to be exceptionally creative. This is likely because what is their weakness in a classroom, a boardroom, a cubicle, or a tedious job is really their strength in a music studio, an art studio, a science lab, or an interesting conversation.

To attain the lofty heights of our society, one most possess nearly-psychotic focus. This focus comes at the cognitive expense of being able to see novel relationships among unrelated concepts. Thoughts that are ostensibly irrelevant to what you are doing when you are focused are weak signals from your unconscious that are trying to say, "what you're doing right now is lame!"

What is bad for time management is good for art. But once you have a creative idea, you need to able to suspend your idea generator in order to focus and get your idea into a physical form. It turns out noise might help you stay in the optimal cognitive range for being creative and concentrating—whether you have ADHD or not.

Recent research by Ravi Mehta, Rui (Juliet) Zhu, and Amar Cheema in the *Journal of Consumer Research* entitled "Is Noise Always Bad? Exploring the Effects of Ambient Noise on Creative Cognition" found that moderate background noise improved subjects' performance on the Remote Associates Test (or RAT), which is a well-established test that psychologists use to measure creative thinking.

The RAT is a relatively simple task, which is similar to the "Ten Thousand Dollar Pyramid" game show where contestants tried to get their partners to guess a word without being allowed to say the word. In the RAT, you are given three or four stimulus words that are in some way related to the "secret" target word. For example, you might be given "shelf," "read," or "end" if the correct word is "book."

Their results show that with moderate background white noise at about seventy decibels, participants were significantly faster at responding to RAT words and gave more correct answers than in low noise or high noise. In other words, moderate noise improves creativity, and a high noise level degrades creativity (as measured by the RAT).

I believe these findings can be perfectly explained by stochastic resonance. I have described how brain regions communicate by synchronizing their oscillations. In this way temporary brain networks are formed to carry out certain functions—like perceiving a scene, listening to a song, or making a PowerPoint presentation.

Through this synchronization, information can spread throughout the network. Adding the right amount of random fluctuation to the system facilitates neural synchronization. Too little noise, and there is not enough synchronization to form a functional network, whereas too much noise can destroy synchronization. Exactly like in the image of Big Ben.

Noise makes the output of downstream neurons synchronize to the frequency of the upstream neurons. At the network level, involving millions of neurons, this noise-induced synchrony mechanism establishes a roughly constant difference between the phases of these weakly-connected oscillators (i.e., neurons). This allows you to have coherent thoughts. Too much synchronization, and you are having a seizure. Not enough, and you aren't thinking at all.

Lawrence Ward is a neuroscientist at the University of British Columbia who is a pioneer in studying stochastic resonance in the human brain. In 2010, he and his colleagues published a groundbreaking study called "Stochastic Resonance Modulates Neural Synchronization within and between Cortical Sources." What this means is that noise influences how groups of neurons synchronize their activity within one brain region, and noise also influences how separate brain regions synchronize with each other.

Several previous studies demonstrated that stochastic resonance likely improves neural synchronization in humans. However, these studies had only been able to show the synchronization in the data from EEG electrodes on the scalp. Therefore, we do not know exactly where in the brain the stochastic resonance effects are occurring. Furthermore, we don't know the extent of the synchronization *within* a brain region.

In a very clever experimental design based on earlier work studying auditory attention, Ward presented streams of sounds to subjects right around their hearing threshold to both ears. The sounds in the left ear were called "left standards," and the sounds in the right ear were called "right standards." At random intervals there were louder sounds mixed into the sound stream called "deviants," which the subject was instructed to respond to by pushing a button whenever they heard the deviant—in the left ear only. These instructions meant that subjects would only pay attention to the sound stream in the left ear and ignore the sounds in their right ears. At the same time, Ward played white noise at different levels in the left ear.

Using the EEG source localization algorithms, Ward found the regions in the brain that were activated by this task, and that were activated in most of his subjects. These brain regions included not only the auditory cortex, but also non-sensory brain regions like the posterior cingulate, which you will remember is part of the default mode network.

Finally, Ward could measure the level of synchronization within and between these brain regions as a function of the noise level he imposed on the left ear of his subjects. The results showed robust stochastic resonance effects on the synchronization within and between brain regions involved in processing auditory signals. In other words, at the right noise level the synchronization between these brain regions was at its peak: the brain responded better to the steady stream of sounds with added noise than without the noise.

I suspect that the neural mechanism that Lawrence Ward identified in his auditory paradigm is just the tip of the iceberg in terms of how the right amount of noise in the environment and inside our brains enhances our cognitive abilities and makes us more creative. His work provides a very plausible biological and physical explanation for the results of similar experiments, such as those I have conducted myself.

Based on my own work with stochastic resonance and ADHD, and from earlier studies on noise and creativity, we know that some types of people require more noise in order to benefit from externally-driven neural stochastic resonance. In particular, individuals who score high on measures of original-ity, creativity, or divergent-thinking seem to perform better on tasks when exposed to higher noise levels.

This is likely related to dopamine function in key brain areas like the prefrontal cortex. Furthermore, it could be that extra noise is necessary in some individuals in order to help functional coherence in the default mode network. Amazingly, none of the psychological work on noise and creativity over the past thirty years has incorporated stochastic resonance. It is remarkable that almost all of these studies unintentionally find psychological or behavioral evidence of stochastic resonance. In other words, if we go back to these studies and model the results using the math of stochastic resonance, the consistent pattern is that a moderate amount of noise improves performance on many tasks. Idleness, then, could turn out to be a way to increase the brain's internal noise level, thus enabling what's called coherence resonance in the default mode network.

Noise that originates inside the system induces order and improves the brain's function, through the same mechanism of stochastic resonance. It could be that working all the time and being busy reduces internal noise to a sub-optimal level. While we still do not have a way to directly measure stochastic resonance inside a living brain, the techniques that Ward is using could be applied to the idle brain and the default mode network.

Let's return to Rilke pacing on the castle battlement by the sea that windy day in northern Italy. The years of patient idleness the poet went through allowed activity in his default mode network to percolate up to his awareness from time to time and so his consciousness was prepared to receive the messages. On that particular morning at Duino, the powerful wind blowing from the sea provided just the right addition of external noise his brain needed to give Rilke the inspiration for one of his life's great works. A highly original and creative person, he would likely have needed more external noise in order for his brain to benefit creatively from stochastic resonance.

Rilke's unconscious had been preparing this poem for him. The poem itself could be considered a weak signal, which as we saw earlier is undetectable without noise. As Rilke walked through the blustery wind that morning, it is possible that the same brain mechanism of noise-enhanced neural synchronization that Lawrence Ward has discovered allowed critical parts of Rilke's brain to synchronize.

This could have formed a functional network that transiently made this great work of poetry appear to Rilke. In the presence of the wind, the weak signal of the poem would then make its way through the network into Rilke's awareness. Furthermore, the strength of the signal would have been boosted over the critical threshold for it to enter into his consciousness. To Rilke, this would have seemed like a voice calling out to him in the wind saying:

And if I cried out, who would hear me up there among the angelic orders?

Lawrence Ward and other scientists are revealing the precise mechanisms by which noise actually helps our brains to achieve some of their most amazing feats of creativity. So rather than fighting noise, or seeing noise as something that distracts us from the truth, we might soon discover that our brains actually require noise to find truth. By embracing idleness, we embrace the noise of our own unconscious. The wind blows inside of us, enabling us to hear the truth in the wind that takes us by surprise, the wind we seek to hear ourselves.

8

SIX SIGMA IS A SEIZURE

"Now I have to tell you something, and I mean this in the best and most inoffensive way possible: I don't believe in process. In fact, when I interview a potential employee and he or she says that 'it's all about the process,' I see that as a bad sign ... The problem is that at a lot of big companies, process becomes a substitute for thinking. You're encouraged to behave like a little gear in a complex machine. Frankly, it allows you to keep people who aren't that smart, who aren't that creative."

—Elon Musk, founder of Space-X and Tesla Motors

If you have a job at any sizable company there is good chance you've been forced to endure Six Sigma training, or at least some watered-down derivative. Your instructor may have reminded you, as mine did, of a newly converted religious fanatic proselytizing his faith. Imagine a cross between a Scientologist and a Jehovah's Witness, tastefully attired in business casual.

Six Sigma devotees refer to their judo belts which denote mastery over the seemingly-infinite levels of the Six Sigma world. You start out as a "green belt" and proceed to a "black belt" if you are a true believer and you work really, really hard. There is also a "Master" level that seems almost unattainable to normal humans.

According to an official account, Six Sigma is an organized and systematic method for strategic process improvement, plus new product and service development, that relies on statistical methods and the scientific method to make dramatic reductions in customer-defined defect rates. Don't worry about trying to understand what that even means: it turns out that not even Ultimate Lean-Master Six Sigma Black Belts understand what it means. Six Sigma is neither statistical nor scientific. You can quite easily get through Six Sigma training by pretending to know what it means, so let's just pretend.

A paper on Six Sigma theory by R. G. Schroeder in the *Journal of Operations Management* from 2008 identifies several definitions: Six Sigma is "a high-performance, data-driven approach to analyzing the root causes of business problems and solving them." Also it's a "business process that allows companies to drastically improve their bottom line by designing and monitoring every business activity in ways that minimize waste and resources while increasing customer satisfaction"; also it's "a disciplined and statistically based approach for improving product and process quality"; also it's "a management strategy that requires culture change in the organization."

After going through a few weeks of Six Sigma training, I basically learned how to write my name on a piece of cardboard, how to draw on flipcharts, and how to pass pieces of paper to other members of my group. All while the instructor gave us questionable information about statistics. I learned too that questioning him about the statistics led to long digressions about his dog in Arizona.

Where did Six Sigma come from? Is it a secret government program gone awry? Legend has it that Six Sigma was developed at Motorola in the early 1980s to study and control defects in semiconductor chip manufacturing—and that's probably where it should have stayed. Unfortunately, like some contagious virus developed at a CDC lab, it escaped the factory. It has now become a horrifying corporate epidemic.

In the 1980s, Motorola wanted to produce perfect semiconductors as fast as possible, while at the same time saving billions of dollars. When you are making semiconductor chips, naturally you want to minimize defects. So once you've worked out the most efficient process to produce your chips, you want to codify the process and make it automatic. Every time a piece of machinery or factory worker does something during the production process, it should happen the exact same way. In other words, there should be no variation in the process. But what does sigma mean? And why is sigma preceded by the number six?

Sigma or "σ" is the Greek letter used in statistics to represent the standard deviation from some mean (the mean is the middle point). Without going into too much detail, the standard deviation represents how much individual measurements differ on average from this mean.

A simple way to illustrate this is with how tall people are. For example, if we measure the height of one thousand male Americans, add up all the heights, and divide by the number of measurements (i.e., one thousand) the average might be around 5'10". So roughly half of the people are shorter and half are taller than 5'10". But we don't know if the average has been calculated because some people are ten feet tall and some two feet tall, or if most people measured hover very close to 5'10".

The standard deviation tells us to what extent most people deviate from this average. Because the population is made up of mostly regular-sized people, height measurements have a small standard deviation of around three inches. Also, because height seems to come from what's called a "normal distribution," also known as a bell curve, height can be studied using traditional statistics.

It's important to note that there are an infinite range of bell curves—not just one distribution called "the bell curve." But by determining both an average and also standard deviation, we can estimate what the heights of the tallest and shortest people are likely to be.

One sigma, or one standard deviation, from the mean with respect to height would cover perhaps sixty-five percent of the people. Since the sigma is three inches, this would refer to people who are either 5'7" on the low end or 6' on the high end. Two sigma from the mean would cover fewer people, perhaps only ten percent, as we move from out from the mean toward the tall and short sides of the spectrum: roughly 6'3" and 5'4."

The farther out in standard deviations from the mean in a normal distribution, the more unusual you are. If you are "Six Sigma" (or six standard deviations) away from the average height you are extremely rare: 7'6." Yao Ming territory. There are only a handful of people in the world who are this tall. The goal of Six Sigma is to make mistakes in business processes as rare as people like Yao Ming.

It's easy to see how this type of thinking can be applied to highly automated processes like manufacturing microchips or cars. You want to engineer your production system to produce faulty cars so rarely that they occur only at Six Sigma frequency. Basically, never.

By analyzing each step of the process and figuring out how to measure inputs and outputs, an average of the process can be taken, just like with measuring height. Then a standard deviation of the process can be worked out. If the standard deviation is very large it means there is too much variation in the process and it has to be changed to produce a smaller standard deviation. In other words, there should be as little variation in the process as possible. The underlying assumption is that variation leads to errors.

However, rather than just using it as a way to standardize production, companies began to apply the Six Sigma approach to every single business process, treating human beings as a series of inputs and outputs instead of sentient creatures. The single most important goal of the Six Sigma is to reduce variation in organizational processes by using disease vectors to spread throughout the company. These vectors are improvement specialists, a structured method, and performance metrics.

This is similar to what the underlying disease in epilepsy does to neurons. During a seizure, the variations in the neurons are reduced. Reducing variation in the brain is devastating.

Applied to an entire company, the Six Sigma process is analogous to an organizational epileptic seizure.

Naturally, if you are making vaccines, aspirin, car parts, airplane engines, MRI scanners, or any other mass-produced thing that could potentially kill people, you want to prevent defects. In these types of highly automated manufacturing processes, Six Sigma makes sense. In fact, it makes sense to use robots to do most manufacturing. For repetitive automated tasks where very little decision-making is required, robots outperform human beings, no question.

Six Sigma wants to make human beings as efficient as possible—predictable, reliable, nearly fault free, and with minimal interference from outside thoughts. Since Jack Welch Six Sigma-ed GE, the approach has spread to many major companies in the industrial sector and beyond. Some of the corporations that are having Six Sigma seizures include Fiat, Honeywell, Dow Chemical, Cameron, Sony, Johnson & Johnson, Bank of America, and Whirlpool.

The human brain actually seeks out and thrives on its own variation. With each new experience we have, our brain is irreversibly changed. These changes become more profound and stable if we rest between new experiences. This allows our brain to consolidate what it has absorbed and integrate it into our own sense of self, therefore making meaning out of experience. The process is different for each experience and different for each person. Neuroscience is discovering that a crucial part of this process is allowing the brain's default mode network time to be active. A resting brain is necessary for this to happen.

Each of our brains has its own rhythm. For example, you can alter it by flying to Europe. After a period of jet lag you will have altered your circadian rhythm to a new time zone. However, once the jet lag has passed, you will have the same daily rhythm that you did in your old time zone. If you are a morning person in New York, you will be a morning person in Paris. This is likely because your brain is generating its own internal pattern, which may be largely inherited.

Our brain responds slightly differently to each situation depending on a great many factors: mood, your fatigue level, and motivation. Our ability to pay attention also has a natural rhythm that waxes and wanes throughout the day. As we've seen, the default mode network's activity likes to oscillate against the task-positive network. When these rhythms of the brain are not allowed to fluctuate naturally, the consequences can be severe for an individual. For example, pilot fatigue is one of the leading causes of airplane crashes.

The natural, nonlinear, fluctuating, and often-unpredictable aspects of human beings are troubling for corporations. CEOs crave certainty and predictability. Throughout the corporate hierarchy, each level must produce high levels of predictability and certainty. Over the last decade or so, the Six Sigma approach has come under intense criticism. Several large companies such as 3M noticed that when they religiously implemented Six Sigma, innovation slowed to a crawl. Michael Tushman, a professor at Harvard Business School, said, "These ... methodologies that are anchored on reducing variability are inversely associated with what we call exploratory innovation. Methodologies help incremental innovation."

Within a decade, the percentage of 3M products that were new or less than five years old slipped from one-third to one-quarter. In other words, before Six Sigma, thirty percent of 3M's products were new, and after Six Sigma, that percentage fell to twenty-five percent. Rather than scrapping Six Sigma, the company stopped using that metric.

Motorola, where the Six Sigma outbreak started, used to enjoy a huge lead in the mobile phone market. Their dominant position in the market has evaporated. The mobile marketplace is one of the fastest moving and most innovative, and it seems like forcing your opponents to adopt Six Sigma tactics is a good way to cripple them.

Capitalist corporations must execute a strange balancing act between two poles on a spectrum that are paradoxical. On the one hand, they must work to the shareholders' immediate benefit—hence Six Sigma. On the other hand, they need ideas for innovative products. Both these contradictory elements are required for the elusive "competitive advantage."

The only system we know of in the universe that can be innovative is the human brain. But the brain seems to need things like freedom, long periods of idleness, positive emotions, low stress, randomness, noise, and a group of friends with tea in the garden to be creative. The truth is that we can't have it both ways. Until we figure out how to give robots a "creative mode," humans are going to be the only source of innovation for the foreseeable future. But the vast majority of business processes do not actually require human thought. Just as many time management strategies admonish you to get things out of your brain and into a physical organizer, Six Sigma would like to minimize human variation within the organization.

Epilepsy kills fifty thousand people a year in the United States alone. About fifty million people around the world have epilepsy, and thirty percent of these people have poorly controlled seizures despite taking the maximum medication dosage. There are many different causes of epilepsy, but the common symptom is having some type of seizure activity. Epilepsy can be inherited or it can be acquired from disease or head trauma. All those concussions you had as a teenager can come back to haunt you. The seizure activity can be very brief and mild like a subtle change in cognitive state.

The patient may not even notice he is having a seizure. You might just "check-out" for a few moments and then rejoin the world without realizing what happened. More serious forms of seizure can cause debilitating convulsions, and in the worst cases death.

Abnormal synchronous neural firing in one or several areas of the brain causes the epilepsy seizure. Recall that the way neurons in your brain communicate is through synchronizing their activity, so that information can flow back and forth between neurons, and between brain regions in the brain network. However, the normal neural synchronization that allows you to be conscious and function is very subtle and relies on groups of neurons that synchronize or desynchronize as necessary. Your everyday cognitive functioning depends on the variation in your neural activity.

Sometimes the synchronization is partial within a patch of brain. This complex interplay of neurons firing together or not together forms the basis of how parts of your brain talk to each other. The process is highly variable, nonlinear, context dependent, noisy, and displays many of the characteristics of complexity and self-organization we see in other complex networks.

In seizure activity, part of the brain becomes what is called hypersynchronous. Hypersynchrony refers to the fact that there is too much synchronization among a group of neurons, or between brain regions. This appears in the EEG record as *ictal* spikes, which look like huge bursts of brain waves all rising and falling together. These can appear at first as low amplitude high frequency waves, which give way to very high amplitude low frequency waves.

What this means is that there is a brain area where all the neurons begin to fire together and do not stop. This hypersynchrony can spread to other brain regions and cause a person to lose consciousness or go into convulsions. In severe and intractable cases, such as when medication does not stop the seizures, neurosurgeons may remove the part of the brain because it will not stop going into hypersynchrony.

Epileptics often feel an "aura" preceding a seizure. This can take many forms from visual hallucinations to brief moments of pure lucidity. Dostoyevsky had epilepsy and described the moments just prior to a seizure as being full of joy and harmony: "For several moments," he said, "I would experience such joy as would be inconceivable in ordinary life—such joy that no one else could have any notion of. I would feel the most complete harmony in myself and in the whole world and this feeling was so strong and sweet that for a few seconds of such bliss I would give ten or more years of my life, even my whole life perhaps."

This type of experience is not uncommon among epileptics, and has in recent decades led scientists to try to predict seizures based on the EEG records from these patients. So far, these efforts have fallen short. This is likely due to the highly variable and nonlinear way in which ictal or seizure activity interacts with normal electrical brain activity, which is also noisy, variable, and nonlinear.

A rigid management strategy is a seizure. One of the chief goals of productivity strategies is to reduce the amount of variation in any company process. When variations in neurons are suppressed too much, and this reduction in variation becomes widespread through hypersynchrony, the result is a seizure that can quickly spread to the rest of the company, causing a global convulsion. The brain can no longer do anything. An organization that is having a seizure stops being creative, adaptive, or any kind of humane place to work.

For example, hiring new people is an important process in any company. A person using the Six Sigma approach would scrutinize this process—creating what's called a process map. Then she would identify wasteful parts of the process. This would involve using things called "Value Stream Mapping" and "Process Flow Tools" to try to identify "value-added" and "non-value-added" parts of the hiring process.

Our Sig Sigma utilizer would likely find that each hiring manager has his or her own way of hiring people—this is called variation, and according to Six Sigma, it's very bad. It leads to a lot of non-value added activities, like having long in-depth conversations with potential new employees. Then, she would develop a process that is as "lean" as possible—i.e., generating no waste.

For example, she might develop a set of standard interview questions that every hiring manager has to learn and use. Thus, the manager could not inject personal noise into the process. Any process that cannot be defined, analyzed, controlled, or improved would be tossed out. Next, she would develop a process for hiring people that is done exactly the same by everyone in the entire organization. In other words, she would make the hiring process something an automated system could do.

She will be able to measure this process and tell if it's working using the same Six Sigma tools used to design it: as though she were measuring a ruler with another ruler. There is no independently verifiable way to know what Six Sigma is doing. So why do companies insist on using it?

Reducing variation is harmful to many natural systems. The ecological consequences of the current vast reduction in global bio-diversity are devastating and we are likely in the midst of a mass extinction. On an individual level, variation in our heart rate is critical to our health. This is tightly connected to our brain's natural variation. Heart rate variability (HRV) is the variation over time in the period between consecutive heartbeats. The HRV reflects your heart's ability to quickly adapt to changing circumstances by detecting unpredictable stimuli. Low HRV means that your risk for stroke or sudden death from cardiac arrest is elevated. Thus, the natural fluctuations in your heart rate are very much connected to your cardiac health. The general rule is that the more nonlinear your heart is, the better your autonomic nervous system is operating.

The purpose of science is to understand reality by trying to disprove theories using experiments. These management fads use concepts and methods that were developed originally within scientific fields, but because they are not used for a scientific end, these torturous methods are misunderstood and misapplied. Science has no goals. Science is a creative act with the same purpose as art: to liberate the human spirit.

9

WORK IS DESTROYING THE PLANET

"The ultimate measure of humanity's success as a species is its ability to increase the overall global output of goods and services by at least five percent per year. The problem is that it is becoming increasingly obvious that if we continue along these lines much longer, we're likely to destroy everything."

—*David Graeber*

"The survival of humans and other species on planet Earth in my view can only be guaranteed via a timely transition towards a stationary state, a world economy without growth."

—*Peter Custers*

This is a well-known phenomenon in psychology called "semantic satiation." For example, say the word "buffalo" to yourself over and over again until you become uncertain about what it means. As you transiently forget what the word "buffalo" means, you might become a little bit scared and think "am I having a stroke?"

The same semantic satiation occurs with the phrase "economic growth." Pick a random newspaper on any day and find the phrase "economic growth" recurring throughout. Economic growth is supposed to mean that we increase the amount of goods and services in the world every year.

Economists use several different metrics to measure this increase of goods and services—the most common of course being the gross domestic product (GDP) which somehow measures how many "goods and services" are created in a particular society or in all the societies on earth combined (called world GDP).[6]

Without economic growth, we are told, billions of people living in extreme poverty would never be able to climb out of poverty, or they would become even poorer. This is despite the fact that by most measures, the number of poor in the world is increasing. To lift them out of poverty, and to avert a global climate catastrophe, we actually need to shrink our economies. But how do we achieve this?

---

[6] As a scientist, I am interested in measuring things. I have been studying measurements for nearly fifteen years. Granted, I'm usually measuring things like brain waves. I am not an economist, though, and when I try (albeit not very hard because it's boring) to understand measurements like the GDP it becomes very clear why. I cannot understand what is really being measured or how it is being measured. For example, we often hear that China has been experiencing exceptional economic growth. China has been increasing its output of goods and services at a rate of about ten percent every year. According to this measurement, every year there are ten percent more goods and services in China than the year before. Does this include things like hamburgers, massages, weddings, and drug dealers? China is also a great example of the theme of this chapter: unchecked economic growth leads to environmental disaster—even in the short term.

Most of the jobs politicians are perpetually promising to create are downright awful. For people without formal education, the countless jobs that each party claims to be able to produce are demeaning and tedious service-sector jobs at places like Amazon fulfillment centers that don't pay enough for rent, healthcare, food, daycare, phone bills, or a car. For people with more formal education there are mindless corporate jobs where the only skill required is to master the asinine business jargon in a way that makes it seem like you are doing something meaningful.

To the ancient Greeks, anyone who had to work to make a living was considered a slave. In modern society almost everyone has to work to make a living because we all owe someone money, or expect a bill to come due in the near future.

Economic growth disproportionately benefits the people who do not need to work—i.e., the people from whom we are ostensibly borrowing our student loans, our mortgages, our car loans, and our credit cards. This group of people includes corporations, politicians who serve the interests of the corporations, and, of course, people who work in international finance.

Consider the financial crisis of 2008. Why were the banks able to cause such widespread misery? They created money out of thin air, loaned it to hapless borrowers, then, when people stopped paying back the fake money, the banks forced the government to pay them the money that they had made up in the first place. They chopped up the debt into microscopic pieces, randomly put some of the pieces back together, and traded all this debt among themselves, creating a gigantic impenetrable web of derivatives and credit default swaps. Why didn't anyone see the crisis coming?

Because people stopped believing in failure. The more we believe in the impossibility of failure, the more likely failure becomes. This is in fact Arthur C. Clarke's first law of prediction: "When a distinguished but elderly scientist states that something is possible, he is almost certainly right. When he states that something is impossible, he is very probably wrong."

I wish to make a radical suggestion: because our social system is predicated on the majority of people believing in the fundamental necessity of work, a sharp increase in idleness, absenteeism, laziness, and non-industriousness might be the most effective way to bring about positive social and political change.

Conjuring Bartleby, a collective "we'd prefer not to" would send much more fear into the hearts of the bankers and CEOs than any organized political movement. Naturally, people need to be able to afford decent housing, food, and health care for themselves and their families. However, the vast majority of jobs in the world simply exist to make a certain group of people more money, thus increasing their relative privilege.

Not only are most people unable to meaningfully choose the nature and intensity of their employment, but once they are employed, they are told by the time management industry that there are correct and incorrect ways to deploy their skills. Then they are told they should be happy about the fact that they have a job at all.

"Smooth shapes are very rare in the wild but extremely important in the ivory tower and the factory."

—*Benoît Mandelbrot*

Recently, *New York Times* columnist Ross Douthat wrote an essay entitled "A World Without Work." "Imagine," he wrote, "as 19th-century utopians often did, a society rich enough that fewer and fewer people need to work—a society where leisure becomes universally accessible, where part-time jobs replace the regimented workweek, and where living standards keep rising even though more people have left the work force altogether. If such a utopia were possible, one might expect that it would be achieved first among the upper class, and then gradually spread down the social ladder."

First of all, Douthat assumes such a utopia is not possible. This is a prime example of what Graeme Webb, a scholar at Simon Fraser University, called the collapse of the social imagination. In a recent paper on how the Occupy movement has reintroduced radicalism to the mainstream, Webb describes the fact that the discourse of individualism, market fundamentalism, and consumerism has come to so dominate our culture that we simply cannot conceive that society can be organized any differently. In our atomized and desperate struggle for individual material well-being, we perceive "that the society we have today is the only possible society; we have lost our imaginations." Webb points out that we have willingly abandoned the idea of utopia, and utopian thinking is denigrated and dismissed.

Secondly, Douthat suggests idle bliss would come to the wealthy ahead of everyone else. Presumably this is because the wealthy are the only ones who have any meaningful choice in the matter. In their magnanimity, according to Douthat, the wealthy would work less and then spread the gift of idleness "down the social ladder." Douthat's trickle-down theory of idleness is presented without irony. His assumption is that the rich have to give the rest of us permission to work less. Revealingly, Douthat seems to be implying that if only wealthy people had the means not to work (as the wealthy do) they wouldn't choose to work. Except, he points out, the wealthy work more than poor people. Nina Easton, a strident apologist for the wealthy at *Fortune*, asked in 2012, "what if I told you that there was a group of hard-driving workaholics who ... bring a level of talent and skill to their jobs that attracts premium pay in the global economy?" According to Douthat, if utopia were possible, these "hard-driving workaholics" would work fewer and fewer hours, and eventually allow their minions—us—to work fewer hours too. Because, you know, rich people are so generous.

The 19th century utopian theorists to whom Douthat refers—Marx, Rousseau, and Fourier—actually thought that the newly-awakened revolutionary working class would usher in utopia and organize society in such a way that work would be beneficial, a source of joy as well as sustenance for all.

Douthat describes the fact that poor people are leaving the job market and surviving without a steady job as "post-employment." The problem, as anthropologist Sarah Kendzior has pointed out, is that "The economic crisis is a crisis of managed expectations. Americans are being conditioned to accept their own exploitation as normal. Ridden with debt from the minute they graduate college, they compete for the privilege of working without pay."

If there is one thing worse than working for pay, it's working without pay. The trick is to create a true post-work society, one that truly liberates human energies. Though the way forward is not immediately apparent, I have faith that the answers are waiting in billions of idle minds, and that the brightest among us have yet to realize that what they really need is a break, a chance to rest, a golden opportunity to do nothing at all.

ACKNOWLEDGEMENTS

"Scholars are ashamed of otium. *But there is something noble about leisure and idleness. If idleness really is the beginning of all vice, then it is at any rate in the closest proximity to all virtue; the idle man is always a better man than the active. But when I speak of leisure and idleness, you do not think I am alluding to you, do you, you sluggards?"*
—*Friedrich Nietzsche*

This book would not have been possible without my amazing wife Sonja Schmer-Galunder. She is my intellectual sparring partner and a great source of ideas. Many of the more ridiculous ideas I had for this book were thankfully shot down by her uncanny logic and insight. She also generously allowed me to work on this book at night and on the weekends while we had two small boys in diapers. She is as much a part of this book as I am.

I also have to thank my own mother Caryl Briscoe. There is not a more selfless person in the universe. My mother always gave me a strong (perhaps delusional) belief in myself, and for this I am very grateful. If this book is audacious, it is in no small part because she helped me believe that I can be daring. This book is also dedicated to her. I watched her dutifully work at a company that used many of the management techniques I attack in this book. My mother coped with the inane and arbitrary continuous performance improvement decrees from the MBA mafia at her job and it made me angry. I like to think of this book partly as my mom's revenge for her years of putting up with the mindless corporate drones at her job.

Thanks to my three beautiful children Marie, Niklas, and Jonas. You are the biggest sources of inspiration and motivation.

Thanks to my sister Sarah Smart for always being there.

I'd like to thank my step-dad and lawyer Frank Briscoe for making me a cyclist, encouraging me to take risks, and for being an immovable concrete base of support during my life. And for letting me try to read Kierkegaard in 8th grade.

I want to thank my workaholic father John Smart and step-mother Holly Smart for your unconditional love and support, for instilling in me an insatiable wanderlust, and for giving me a fascination with gigantic machinery.

I need to thank my screenwriting partner and BFF Arya Senboutaraj for being a great inspiration, for my portrait, and for always encouraging me to go for it. We'll get there.

I owe an enormous philosophical, political, emotional, and practical debt to Anthony Troy Fiscella, without whom this book would have been little more than a few loosely connected thoughts. Well, it still might be just a few loosely connected thoughts, but because of Troy's honesty and critical mind there are hundreds of research papers behind these thoughts. I have to thank my lab mates Trent Reusser and Stephen Whitlow for making our work environment tolerable and even a lot of fun, and for teaching me how to program.

I'd like to thank Leyla Kader Dahm for providing guidance for a naïve writer. I owe Sarah Douglas, cultural editor at the New York *Observer*, for introducing me to Rilke in high school and for being a friend since we were twelve.

My path to the science of idleness has been a long and circuitous one and I want to thank the scientists who have personally influenced me over the years: Jonathan Friedman, David Graeber, Steven Sampson, Sverker Sikström, Petter Kallioinen, Kristoffer Åberg, Jonas Olofsson, Scott Makeig, Rey Ramirez, Liina Pylkkänen, Hakwan Lau, Stanislas Dehaene, and Santosh Mathan.

Finally, the most important thanks for making this book a reality goes to John Oakes at OR Books. John responded to my initial query email summarizing the idea for this book with: "wow." He has been immensely encouraging throughout the process of writing and a huge source of inspiration. I am so honored and proud to be associated with such a great publisher.

REFERENCES

Allen, David. *Getting Things Done: The Art of Stress-Free Productivity.* First Thus. Penguin Books, 2002.

Altamura, Mario, Brita Elvevåg, Gaetano Campi, Michela De Salvia, Daniele Marasco, Alessandro Ricci, and Antonello Bellomo. "Toward Scale-free Like Behavior Under Increasing Cognitive Load." *Complexity* 18, no. 1 (2012): 38–43. doi:10.1002/cplx.21407.

Altenmüller, Eckart, Mario Wiesendanger, and Jurg Kesselring. *Music, Motor Control and the Brain.* Oxford University Press, 2006. http://www.oxfordscholarship.com/view/10.1093/acprof:oso/9780199298723.001.0001/acprof-9780199298723.

Anticevic, Alan, Michael W. Cole, John D. Murray, Philip R. Corlett, Xiao-Jing Wang, and John H. Krystal. "The Role of Default Network Deactivation in Cognition and Disease." *Trends in Cognitive Sciences* 16, no. 12 (December 2012): 584–592. doi:10.1016/j.tics.2012.10.008.

Arden, Rosalind, Robert S. Chavez, Rachael Grazioplene, and Rex E. Jung. "Neuroimaging Creativity: A Psychometric View." *Behavioural Brain Research* 214, no. 2 (December 25, 2010): 143–156. doi:10.1016/j.bbr.2010.05.015.

"Are Ants Vulnerable to Climate Change?" *East Tennessean.* Accessed November 1, 2012. http://www.easttennessean.com/news/are-ants-vulnerable-to-climate-change-1.2860631#.UJLXiIa9zWc.

Barton, C. Michael, Isaac I.T. Ullah, Sean M. Bergin, Helena Mitasova, and Hessam Sarjoughian. "Looking for the Future in the Past: Long-term

Change in Socioecological Systems." *Ecological Modelling* 241 (August 24, 2012): 42–53. doi:10.1016/j.ecolmodel.2012.02.010.

Benner, Mary J., and Michael L. Tushman. "Exploitation, Exploration, and Process Management: The Productivity Dilemma Revisited." *The Academy of Management Review* 28, no. 2 (April 1, 2003): 238–256. doi:10.2307/30040711.

Benzi, Roberto. "Stochastic Resonance: From Climate to Biology." *arXiv:nlin/0702008* (February 5, 2007). http://arxiv.org/abs/nlin/0702008.

Binnewijzend, Maja A.A., Menno M. Schoonheim, Ernesto Sanz-Arigita, Alle Meije Wink, Wiesje M. van der Flier, Nelleke Tolboom, Sofie M. Adriaanse, et al. "Resting-state fMRI Changes in Alzheimer's Disease and Mild Cognitive Impairment." *Neurobiology of Aging* 33, no. 9 (September 2012): 2018–2028. doi:10.1016/j.neurobiolaging.2011.07.003.

Blanchard, Kenneth H., and Spencer Johnson. *The One Minute Manager.* William Morrow, 2003.

Bohm, David. *On Creativity.* 2nd ed. Routledge, 2004.

Bronson, Po, and Ashley Merryman. "THE CREATIVITY CRISIS. (Cover Story)." *Newsweek* 156, no. 3 (July 19, 2010): 44–49.

Brown, P., and P. Warner-Smith. "The Taylorisation of family time: an effective strategy in the struggle to 'manage' work and life?" *Annals of Leisure Research* 8, no. 2/3 (2005): 75–90.

Buckner, Randy L., and Justin L. Vincent. "Unrest at Rest: Default Activity and Spontaneous Network Correlations." *NeuroImage* 37, no. 4 (October 1, 2007): 1091–1096. doi:10.1016/j.neuroimage.2007.01.010.

Bullmore, Ed, and Olaf Sporns. "Complex Brain Networks: Graph Theoretical Analysis of Structural and Functional Systems." *Nature Reviews Neuroscience* 10, no. 3 (March 1, 2009): 186.

Buzsaki, Gyorgy. *Rhythms of the Brain.* 1st ed. Oxford University Press, USA, 2011.

Cagliuso Sr., Nicholas V. "The Risks of Terrorism." *Journal of Homeland Security and Emergency Management* 2, no. 2 (June 14, 2005): 1–5. doi:10.2202/1547-7355.1129.

Cairney, Paul. "Complexity Theory in Political Science and Public Policy." *Political Studies Review* 10, no. 3 (2012): 346–358. doi:10.1111/j.1478-9302.2012.00270.x.

Carhart-Harris, R. L., and K. J. Friston. "The Default-mode, Ego-functions and Free-energy: a Neurobiological Account of Freudian Ideas." *Brain* 133, no. 4 (April 1, 2010): 1265–1283. doi:10.1093/brain/awq010.

Charlton, Bruce G. "The Busy Shall Inherit the Earth: The Evolution from 'Hard Work' to 'Busyness' in Modern Science and Society." *Medical Hypotheses* 67, no. 5 (2006): 1003–1005. doi:10.1016/j.mehy.2006.04.001.

Colonnese, Matthew, and Rustem Khazipov. "Spontaneous Activity in Developing Sensory Circuits: Implications for Resting State fMRI." *NeuroImage* 62, no. 4 (October 1, 2012): 2212–2221. doi:10.1016/j.neuroimage.2012.02.046.

"Complexity at Large." *Complexity* 17, no. 6 (2012): 1–4. doi:10.1002/cplx.21404.

Custers, Peter. "The Tasks of Keynesianism Today: Green New Deals As Transition Towards a Zero Growth Economy?" *New Political Science* 32, no. 2 (June 2010): 173–191.

D'Argembeau, Arnaud, Fabienne Collette, Martial Van der Linden, Steven Laureys, Guy Del Fiore, Christian Degueldre, André Luxen, and Eric Salmon. "Self-referential Reflective Activity and Its Relationship with Rest: a PET Study." *NeuroImage* 25, no. 2 (April 1, 2005): 616–624. doi:10.1016/j.neuroimage.2004.11.048.

Das, Pritha, Vince Calhoun, and Gin S. Malhi. "Mentalizing in Male Schizophrenia Patients Is Compromised by Virtue of Dysfunctional Connectivity Between Task-positive and Task-negative Networks." *Schizophrenia Research* 140, no. 1–3 (September 2012): 51–58. doi:10.1016/j.schres.2012.06.023.

Deco, Gustavo, Edmund T. Rolls, and Ranulfo Romo. "Stochastic Dynamics as a Principle of Brain Function." *Progress in Neurobiology* 88, no. 1 (May 2009): 1–16. doi:10.1016/j.pneurobio.2009.01.006.

Dehaene, Stanislas. *Reading in the Brain: The Science and Evolution of a Human Invention.* 1st ed. Viking Adult, 2009.

Dennett, Daniel C. *Freedom Evolves.* Reprint. Penguin Books, 2004.

Di Simplicio, M, R Norbury, and C J Harmer. "Short-term Antidepressant Administration Reduces Negative Self-referential Processing in the Medial Prefrontal Cortex in Subjects at Risk for Depression." *Molecular Psychiatry* 17, no. 5 (March 1, 2011): 503–510. doi:10.1038/mp.2011.16.

Douthat, Ross. "A World Without Work." *The New York Times*, February 23, 2013, sec. Opinion / Sunday Review. http://www.nytimes.com/2013/02/24/opinion/sunday/douthat-a-world-without-work.html.

Doyle, Maddie, and Adrian Furnham. "The Distracting Effects of Music on the Cognitive Test Performance of Creative and Non-creative Individuals." *Thinking Skills and Creativity* 7, no. 1 (April 2012): 1–7. doi:10.1016/j. tsc.2011.09.002.

"The Dramatic Rise of Anxiety and Depression in Children and Adolescents: Is It Connected to the Decline in Play and Rise in Schooling?" Accessed October 16, 2012. http://www.psychologytoday.com/blog/freedom-learn/201001/the-dramatic-rise-anxiety-and-depression-in-children-and-adolescents-is-it.

Durr, Volker. "[untitled]." *The German Quarterly* 78, no. 1 (December 1, 2005): 114–115.

Eastwood, John D., Alexandra Frischen, Mark J. Fenske, and Daniel Smilek. "The Unengaged Mind Defining Boredom in Terms of Attention." *Perspectives on Psychological Science* 7, no. 5 (September 1, 2012): 482–495. doi:10.1177/1745691612456044.

"Elon Musk's Mission to Mars | Wired Science | Wired.com." *Wired Science.* Accessed November 16, 2012. http://www.wired.com/wiredscience/2012/10/ff-elon-musk-qa/.

Farnsworth, Keith D., Olga Lyashevska, and Tak Fung. "Functional Complexity: The Source of Value in Biodiversity." *Ecological Complexity* 11 (September 2012): 46–52. doi:10.1016/j.ecocom.2012.02.001.

Fleck, J.I., and J. Kounios. "Intuition, Creativity, and Unconscious Aspects of Problem Solving." In *Encyclopedia of Consciousness*, 431–446. Oxford: Academic Press, 2009. http://www.sciencedirect.com/science/article/pii/B9780123738738000426.

Foster, Brett L., Mohammad Dastjerdi, and Josef Parvizi. "Neural Populations in Human Posteromedial Cortex Display Opposing Responses During Memory and Numerical Processing." *Proceedings of the National Academy of Sciences* 109, no. 38 (September 18, 2012): 15514–15519. doi:10.1073/pnas.1206580109.

Frank, Bernhard. "Rilke's the Panther." *The Explicator* 61, no. 1 (2002): 31–33. doi:10.1080/00144940209597744.

Friston, Karl. "The History of the Future of the Bayesian Brain." *NeuroImage* 62, no. 2 (August 15, 2012): 1230–1233. doi:10.1016/j.neuroimage.2011.10.004.

Friston, Karl, Michael Breakspear, and Gustavo Deco. "Perception and Self-organized Instability." *Frontiers in Computational Neuroscience* 6 (2012). doi:10.3389/fncom.2012.00044.

Gaffrey, Michael S., Joan L. Luby, Kelly Botteron, Grega Repovš, and Deanna M. Barch. "Default Mode Network Connectivity in Children with a History of Preschool Onset Depression." *Journal of Child Psychology and Psychiatry* 53, no. 9 (2012): 964–972. doi:10.1111/j.1469-7610.2012.02552.x.

Giorgio Zuffo, Riccardo. "Taylor Is Dead, Hurray Taylor! The 'Human Factor' in Scientific Management: Between Ethics, Scientific Psychology and Common Sense." *Journal of Business & Management* 17, no. 1 (April 2011): 23–41.

Glackin, Cornelius, Liam Maguire, Liam McDaid, and John Wade. "Synchrony: A Spiking-based Mechanism for Processing Sensory Stimuli." *Neural Networks* 32 (August 2012): 26–34. doi:10.1016/j.neunet.2012.02.020.

Gordon, Evan M., Melanie Stollstorff, Joseph M. Devaney, Stephanie Bean, and Chandan J. Vaidya. "Effect of Dopamine Transporter Genotype on Intrinsic Functional Connectivity Depends on Cognitive State." *Cerebral Cortex* 22, no. 9 (September 1, 2012): 2182–2196. doi:10.1093/cercor/bhr305.

Grabow, Carsten, Stefan Grosskinsky, and Marc Timme. "Small-World Network Spectra in Mean-Field Theory." *Physical Review Letters* 108, no. 21 (May 21, 2012): 218701. doi:10.1103/PhysRevLett.108.218701.

Graeber, David. *Debt: The First 5,000 Years.* First Edition. Melville House, 2011.

Grauwin, Sebastian, Guillaume Beslon, Éric Fleury, Sara Franceschelli, Celine Robardet, Jean-Baptiste Rouquier, and Pablo Jensen. "Complex Systems Science: Dreams of Universality, Interdisciplinarity Reality." *Journal of the American Society for Information Science and Technology* 63, no. 7 (2012): 1327–1338. doi:10.1002/asi.22644.

Guerin, Daniel, ed. *No Gods No Masters: An Anthology of Anarchism.* AK Press, 2005.

Gusnard, Debra A., Erbil Akbudak, Gordon L. Shulman, and Marcus E. Raichle. "Medial Prefrontal Cortex and Self-referential Mental Activity: Relation to a Default Mode of Brain Function." *Proceedings of the National Academy of Sciences* 98, no. 7 (March 27, 2001): 4259–4264. doi:10.1073/pnas.071043098.

Hamilton, J. Paul, Michael C. Chen, and Ian H. Gotlib. "Neural Systems Approaches to Understanding Major Depressive Disorder: An Intrinsic Functional Organization Perspective." *Neurobiology of Disease* (February 2012). doi:10.1016/j.nbd.2012.01.015.

Hamilton, Tyler, and Daniel Coyle. *The Secret Race: Inside the Hidden World of the Tour De France: Doping, Cover-ups, and Winning at All Costs.* First Edition. Bantam, 2012.

Harrison, Lawrence E., and Samuel P. Huntington. *Culture Matters: How Values Shape Human Progress.* Basic Books, 2001.

Hodgkinson, Tom. *How to Be Idle: A Loafer's Manifesto.* First Edition. Harper Perennial, 2007.

Hölldobler, Bert, and Edward O. Wilson. *The Superorganism: The Beauty, Elegance, and Strangeness of Insect Societies.* 1st ed. W. W. Norton & Company, 2008.

Hsee, Christopher K, Adelle X Yang, and Liangyan Wang. "Idleness Aversion and the Need for Justifiable Busyness." *Psychological Science* 21, no. 7 (July 2010): 926–930. doi:10.1177/0956797610374738.

Immordino-Yang, Mary Helen, Joanna A. Christodoulou, and Vanessa Singh. "Rest Is Not Idleness: Implications of the Brain's Default Mode for Human Development and Education." *Perspectives on Psychological Science* 7, no. 4 (July 1, 2012): 352–364. doi:10.1177/1745691612447308.

"The Importance of Scheduling Downtime." *Stepcase Lifehack.* Accessed August 20, 2012. http://www.lifehack.org/articles/productivity/the-importance-of-scheduling-downtime.html.

Isaeva, V. V. "Self-organization in Biological Systems." *Biology Bulletin* 39, no. 2 (March 27, 2012): 110–118. doi:10.1134/S1062359012020069.

Jager B. "Rilkes 'Archaic Torso of Apollo.'" *Journal of Phenomenological Psychology* 34, no. 1 (2003): 79–98. doi:10.1163/156916203322484833.

Jakob, Michael, Gunnar Luderer, Jan Steckel, Massimo Tavoni, and Stephanie Monjon. "Time to Act Now? Assessing the Costs of Delaying Climate Measures and Benefits of Early Action." *Climatic Change* 114, no. 1 (2012): 79–99. doi:10.1007/s10584-011-0128-3.

Johnson, Samuel, and Walter Jackson Bate. *The Yale edition of the works of Samuel Johnson. 2, The Idler and The Adventurer.* New Haven: Yale U.P., 1963.

Jullien, Francois. *Treatise on Efficacy: Between Western and Chinese Thinking.* University of Hawaii Press, 2004.

Jung, Peter, and Fabio Marchesoni. "Energetics of Stochastic Resonance." *Chaos* 21, no. 4 (December 2011): 047516.

Jung, Tzyy-Ping, Scott Makeig, Martin J. McKeown, Anthony J. Bell, Te-Won Lee, and Terrence J. Sejnowski. "Imaging Brain Dynamics Using Independent Component Analysis." *Proceedings of the IEEE. Institute of Electrical and Electronics Engineers* 89, no. 7 (July 1, 2001): 1107–1122. doi:10.1109/5.939827.

Keller, Klaus, Benjamin M. Bolker, and David F. Bradford. "Uncertain Climate Thresholds and Optimal Economic Growth." *Journal of Environmental Economics and Management* 48, no. 1 (July 2004): 723–741. doi:10.1016/j.jeem.2003.10.003.

Killgore, William D. S., Zachary J. Schwab, and Melissa R. Weiner. "Self-reported Nocturnal Sleep Duration Is Associated with Next-day Resting State Functional Connectivity." *NeuroReport* 23, no. 13 (September 2012): 741–745. doi:10.1097/WNR.0b013e3283565056.

Kim, Dong-Youl, and Jong-Hwan Lee. "Are Posterior Default-mode Networks More Robust Than Anterior Default-mode Networks? Evidence from Resting-state fMRI Data Analysis." *Neuroscience Letters* 498, no. 1 (July 1, 2011): 57–62. doi:10.1016/j.neulet.2011.04.062.

Klingberg, Torkel. *The Overflowing Brain:Information Overload and the Limits of Working Memory.* Oxford University Press, 2008.

Kosko, Bart. *Noise.* First Edition. Viking Adult, 2006.

Kounios, John, and Mark Beeman. "The Aha! Moment The Cognitive Neuroscience of Insight." *Current Directions in Psychological Science* 18, no. 4 (August 1, 2009): 210–216. doi:10.1111/j.1467-8721.2009.01638.x.

Kramer, Mark A., and Sydney S. Cash. "Epilepsy as a Disorder of Cortical Network Organization." *The Neuroscientist* 18, no. 4 (August 1, 2012): 360–372. doi:10.1177/1073858411422754.

Kwapień, Jarosław, and Stanisław Drożdż. "Physical Approach to Complex Systems." *Physics Reports* 515, no. 3–4 (June 2012): 115–226. doi:10.1016/j.physrep.2012.01.007.

Lang, Les. "Obesity Threatens U.S. Life Expectancy." *Gastroenterology* 128, no. 5 (May 2005): 1156. doi:10.1053/j.gastro.2005.04.004.

Lesjak, Carolyn. "Utopia, Use, and the Everyday: Oscar Wilde and a New Economy of Pleasure." *ELH* 67, no. 1 (April 1, 2000): 179–204.

Liang, Zhifeng, Jean King, and Nanyin Zhang. "Anticorrelated Resting-state Functional Connectivity in Awake Rat Brain." *NeuroImage* 59, no. 2 (January 16, 2012): 1190–1199. doi:10.1016/j.neuroimage.2011.08.009.

Luu, Phan, and Michael I. Posner. "Anterior Cingulate Cortex Regulation of Sympathetic Activity." *Brain* 126, no. 10 (October 1, 2003): 2119–2120. doi:10.1093/brain/awg257.

Maleyeff, John, Edward A. Arnheiter, and Venkat Venkateswaran. "The Continuing Evolution of Lean Six Sigma." *The TQM Journal* 24, no. 6 (September 28, 2012): 542–555. doi:10.1108/17542731211270106.

Marchetti, Igor, Ernst H. W. Koster, Edmund J. Sonuga-Barke, and Rudi Raedt. "The Default Mode Network and Recurrent Depression: A Neurobiological Model of Cognitive Risk Factors." *Neuropsychology Review* 22, no. 3 (May 9, 2012): 229–251. doi:10.1007/s11065-012-9199-9.

McDonnell, Mark Damian, Nigel G. Stocks, Charles Edward Miller Pearce, and Derek Abbott. "Stochastic Resonance: from Suprathreshold Stochastic Resonance to Stochastic Signal Quantization." Cambridge University Press, 2008.

Mehta, Ravi, Zhu, and Amar Cheema. "Is Noise Always Bad? Exploring the Effects of Ambient Noise on Creative Cognition." *Journal of Consumer Research* 39, no. 4 (December 1, 2012): 784–799. doi:10.1086/665048.

Mikutta, Christian, Andreas Altorfer, Werner Strik, and Thomas Koenig. "Emotions, Arousal, and Frontal Alpha Rhythm Asymmetry During Beethoven's 5th Symphony." *Brain Topography* 25, no. 4 (2012): 423–430. doi:10.1007/s10548-012-0227-0.

Minkel, Jared D., Siobhan Banks, Oo Htaik, Marisa C. Moreta, Christopher W. Jones, Eleanor L. McGlinchey, Norah S. Simpson, and David F. Dinges. "Sleep Deprivation and Stressors: Evidence for Elevated Negative Affect in Response to Mild Stressors When Sleep Deprived." *Emotion* (2012). doi:10.1037/a0026871.

Mörtl, Alexander, Tamara Lorenz, Björn N. S. Vlaskamp, Azwirman Gusrialdi, Anna Schubö, and Sandra Hirche. "Modeling Inter-human Movement Coordination: Synchronization Governs Joint Task Dynamics." *Biological Cybernetics* 106, no. 4–5 (May 31, 2012): 241–259. doi:10.1007/s00422-012-0492-8.

Nath, Biman, and Bikram Phookun. "Dark Matter." *Resonance* 10, no. 12 (December 1, 2005): 76–82. doi:10.1007/BF02835131.

Nesbit, Molly. "Last Words (Rilke, Wittgenstein) (Duchamp)." *Art History* 21, no. 4 (1998): 546–564. doi:10.1111/1467-8365.00129.

Ngai, Pun, and Jenny Chan. "Global Capital, the State, and Chinese Workers: The Foxconn Experience." *Modern China* 38, no. 4 (July 1, 2012): 383–410. doi:10.1177/0097700412447164.

Nisbet, J. F. "Philosophical and Scientific Genius." In *The Insanity of Genius and the General Inequality of Human Faculty Physiologically Considered (6th Ed.)*, 216–253. New York, NY: Charles Scribner's Sons, 1912.

Pagel, J. F. "The Synchronous Electrophysiology of Conscious States." *Dreaming* 22, no. 3 (2012): 173–191. doi:10.1037/a0029659.

Palva, J. Matias, and Satu Palva. "Infra-slow Fluctuations in Electrophysiological Recordings, Blood-oxygenation-level-dependent Signals, and Psychophysical Time Series." *NeuroImage* 62, no. 4 (October 1, 2012): 2201–2211. doi:10.1016/j.neuroimage.2012.02.060.

Paton, Steve. "Introducing Taylor to the Knowledge Economy." *Employee Relations* 35, no. 1 (November 9, 2012): 20–38. doi:10.1108/01425451311279393.

Pfeifer, Rolf, Max Lungarella, and Fumiya Iida. "Self-Organization, Embodiment, and Biologically Inspired Robotics." *Science* 318, no. 5853 (November 16, 2007): 1088–1093. doi:10.1126/science.1145803.

"Position brief_AIRCRAFT_NOISE_2009.pdf." Accessed December 8, 2012. http://www.aci.aero/aci/aci/file/Position%20Briefs/position%20brief_AIRCRAFT_NOISE_2009.pdf.

Pozen, Robert C. *Extreme Productivity: Boost Your Results, Reduce Your Hours.* HarperBusiness, 2012.

Prater, Donald. *A Ringing Glass.* Oxford University Press, 1994. http://www.oxfordscholarship.com.ludwig.lub.lu.se/view/10.1093/acprof:oso/9780198158912.001.0001/acprof-9780198158912.

Raichle, Marcus E. "A Paradigm Shift in Functional Brain Imaging." *The Journal of Neuroscience* 29, no. 41 (October 14, 2009): 12729–12734. doi:10.1523/JNEUROSCI.4366-09.2009.

———. "Intrinsic Activity and Consciousness." In *Characterizing Consciousness: From Cognition to the Clinic?*, edited by Stanislas Dehaene and Yves Christen, 147–160. Research and Perspectives in Neurosciences. Springer

Berlin Heidelberg, 2011. http://www.springerlink.com.ludwig.lub.lu.se/content/v312t865273632r5/abstract/.

———. "The Brain's Dark Energy." *Science* 314, no. 5803 (November 24, 2006): 1249–1250.

———. "The Restless Brain." *Brain Connectivity* 1, no. 1 (January 2011): 3–12. doi:10.1089/brain.2011.0019.

Riley, Michael A., and M. T. Turvey. "The Self-Organizing Dynamics of Intentions and Actions." *The American Journal of Psychology* 114, no. 1 (April 1, 2001): 160–169. doi:10.2307/1423388.

Rilke, Rainer Maria. *Selected Poems of Rainer Maria Rilke.* New edition. Harper Perennial, 1981.

———. *The Selected Poetry of Rainer Maria Rilke.* Translated and edited by Stephen Mitchell. Bilingual Edition: English and German. Vintage, 1989.

Roberts, Alasdair. "Why the Occupy Movement Failed." *Public Administration Review* 72, no. 5 (2012): 754–762. doi:10.1111/j.1540-6210.2012.02614.x.

Robinson, Andrew, and Simon Tormey. "Beyond the State: Anthropology and 'Actually-existing-anarchism.'" *Critique of Anthropology* 32, no. 2 (June 1, 2012): 143–157. doi:10.1177/0308275X12438779.

Ronald Burke, Lisa Fiksenbaum. "Work Motivations, Work Outcomes, and Health: Passion Versus Addiction." *Journal of Business Ethics* 84, no. 2 (2009): 257–263.

Rosales, Jon. "Crecimiento Económico, Cambio Climático, Pérdida De Biodiversidad: Justicia Distributiva Para El Norte y El Sur." *Conservation Biology* 22, no. 6 (2008): 1409–1417. doi:10.1111/j.1523-1739.2008.01091.x.

Russell, Bertrand. *In Praise of Idleness: And Other Essays.* 2nd ed. Routledge, 2004.

Russell, David F., Lon A. Wilkens, and Frank Moss. "Use of Behavioural Stochastic Resonance by Paddle Fish for Feeding." *Nature* 402, no. 6759 (November 18, 1999): 291–294. doi:10.1038/46279.

Sanjuán, Miguel A.F. "Stochastic Resonance. From Suprathreshold Stochastic Resonance to Stochastic Signal Quantization, by M.D. McDonnell, N.G. Stocks, C.E.M. Pearce and D. Abbott." *Contemporary Physics* 51, no. 5 (2010): 448–449. doi:10.1080/00107510903318814.

Sasai, Shuntaro, Fumitaka Homae, Hama Watanabe, Akihiro T. Sasaki, Hiroki C. Tanabe, Norihiro Sadato, and Gentaro Taga. "A NIRS–fMRI Study of

Resting State Network." *NeuroImage* 63, no. 1 (October 15, 2012): 179–193. doi:10.1016/j.neuroimage.2012.06.011.

Sayama, Hiroki. "Morphologies of Self-organizing Swarms in 3D Swarm Chemistry." In *Proceedings of the Fourteenth International Conference on Genetic and Evolutionary Computation Conference*, 577–584. GECCO '12. New York, NY, USA: ACM, 2012. doi:10.1145/2330163.2330245.

Schermer, Victor L. "Group-as-a-Whole and Complexity Theories: Areas of Convergence. Part I: Background and Literature Review." *Group Analysis* 45, no. 3 (September 1, 2012): 275–288. doi:10.1177/0533316412453701.

Schlee, Winfried, Vera Leirer, Stephan Kolassa, Franka Thurm, Thomas Elbert, and Iris-Tatjana Kolassa. "Development of Large-scale Functional Networks over the Lifespan." *Neurobiology of Aging* 33, no. 10 (October 2012): 2411–2421. doi:10.1016/j.neurobiolaging.2011.11.031.

Schroeder, Roger G., Kevin Linderman, Charles Liedtke, and Adrian S. Choo. "Six Sigma: Definition and Underlying Theory." *Journal of Operations Management* 26, no. 4 (July 2008): 536–554. doi:10.1016/j.jom.2007.06.007.

Scott, James C. *Seeing Like a State: How Certain Schemes to Improve the Human Condition Have Failed*. New edition. Yale University Press, 1999.

Scoville, James G. "The Taylorization of Vladimir Ilich Lenin." *Industrial Relations* 40, no. 4 (October 2001): 620.

Sequeira, Sonia. "Randomness and Creativity." *Trends in Neurosciences* 24, no. 12 (December 1, 2001): 694. doi:10.1016/S0166-2236(00)02081-6.

Serge, Victor. *Memoirs of a Revolutionary*. Edited by Richard Greeman. Translated by Peter Sedgwick and George Paizis. NYRB Classics, 2012.

Shelhamer, Mark. *Nonlinear Dynamics in Physiology: A State-space Approach*. World Scientific Publishing Company, 2006.

Sikström, Sverker, and Göran Söderlund. "Stimulus-dependent Dopamine Release in Attention-deficit/hyperactivity Disorder." *Psychological Review* 114, no. 4 (2007): 1047–1075. doi:10.1037/0033-295X.114.4.1047.

Silver, Nate. *The Signal and the Noise: Why Most Predictions Fail but Some Don't*. 1st ed. Penguin Press HC, 2012.

Smith, Adam. *The Wealth of Nations*. Thrifty Books, 2009.

Smith, Daniel Sandford. "Newton's Apple." *Physics Education* 32, no. 2 (March 1997): 129–131. doi:10.1088/0031-9120/32/2/024.

Söderlund, Göran, Sverker Sikström, and Andrew Smart. "Listen to the Noise: Noise Is Beneficial for Cognitive Performance in ADHD." *Journal of Child Psychology & Psychiatry* 48, no. 8 (August 2007): 840–847.

"Statistics for Psychology 5th Edition by Aron | 0136010571 | 9780136010579 | Chegg.com." Accessed December 31, 2012. http://www.chegg.com/textbooks/statistics-for-psychology-5th-edition-9780136010579-0136010571.

Steger, Michael F., Bryan J. Dik, and Ryan D. Duffy. "Measuring Meaningful Work The Work and Meaning Inventory (WAMI)." *Journal of Career Assessment* 20, no. 3 (August 1, 2012): 322–337. doi:10.1177/1069072711436160.

Stella, Federico, Erika Cerasti, Bailu Si, Karel Jezek, and Alessandro Treves. "Self-organization of Multiple Spatial and Context Memories in the Hippocampus." *Neuroscience & Biobehavioral Reviews* 36, no. 7 (August 2012): 1609–1625. doi:10.1016/j.neubiorev.2011.12.002.

"Super-active Students Are Over-scheduled | Harvard Magazine Mar-Apr 2010." Accessed December 4, 2012. http://harvardmagazine.com/2010/03/nonstop.

Sylvester, C.M., M. Corbetta, M.E. Raichle, T.L. Rodebaugh, B.L. Schlaggar, Y.I. Sheline, C.F. Zorumski, and E.J. Lenze. "Functional Network Dysfunction in Anxiety and Anxiety Disorders." *Trends in Neurosciences* 35, no. 9 (September 2012): 527–535. doi:10.1016/j.tins.2012.04.012.

Thompson, Edmund R., and Florence T. T. Phua. "A Brief Index of Affective Job Satisfaction." *Group & Organization Management* 37, no. 3 (June 1, 2012): 275–307. doi:10.1177/1059601111434201.

Timimi, Sami. "Rethinking Childhood Depression." *BMJ: British Medical Journal* 329, no. 7479 (December 11, 2004): 1394–1396.

Toplyn, Glenn Allen. "The Differential Effect of Noise on Creative Task Performance." Ph.D., St. John's University (New York), 1987. http://search.proquest.com.ludwig.lub.lu.se/docview/303608665.

Uddin, Lucina Q., A.M. Clare Kelly, Bharat B. Biswal, Daniel S. Margulies, Zarrar Shehzad, David Shaw, Manely Ghaffari, et al. "Network Homogeneity Reveals Decreased Integrity of Default-mode Network in ADHD." *Journal of Neuroscience Methods* 169, no. 1 (March 30, 2008): 249–254. doi:10.1016/j.jneumeth.2007.11.031.

Ward, Lawrence M., Shannon E. MacLean, and Aaron Kirschner. "Stochastic Resonance Modulates Neural Synchronization Within and Between

Cortical Sources." *PLoS ONE* 5, no. 12 (December 16, 2010): e14371. doi:10.1371/journal.pone.0014371.

Ward, Patrick, and Gerald Shively, "Vulnerability, Income Growth and Climate Change." *World Development* 40, no. 5 (May 2012): 916–927. doi:10.1016/j.worlddev.2011.11.015.

Webb, Graeme. "'Occupying' Our Social Imagination: The Necessity of Utopian Discourses in an Anti-Utopian Age." *Perspectives on Global Development & Technology* 12, no. 1/2 (January 2013): 152–161.

Wellens, Thomas, Vyacheslav Shatokhin, and Andreas Buchleitner. "Stochastic Resonance." *Reports on Progress in Physics* 67, no. 1 (January 1, 2004): 45–105. doi:10.1088/0034-4885/67/1/R02.

Wong, Chi Wah, Valur Olafsson, Omer Tal, and Thomas T. Liu. "Anti-correlated Networks, Global Signal Regression, and the Effects of Caffeine in Resting-state Functional MRI." *NeuroImage* 63, no. 1 (October 15, 2012): 356–364. doi:10.1016/j.neuroimage.2012.06.035.

"ZCommunications | On Media, Healthcare, Economics, Jobs, Dangers of Human Intelligence, Part I by Noam Chomsky | ZNet Article." Accessed December 10, 2012. http://www.zcommunications.org/on-media-healthcare-economics-jobs-dangers-of-human-intelligence-part-i-by-noam-chomsky.

Zemanová, Lucia, Gorka Zamora-López, Changsong Zhou, and Jürgen Kurths. "Complex Brain Networks: From Topological Communities to Clustered Dynamics." *Pramana* 70, no. 6 (June 1, 2008): 1087–1097. doi:10.1007/s12043-008-0113-1.

Zemanová, Lucia, Changsong Zhou, and Jürgen Kurths. "Structural and Functional Clusters of Complex Brain Networks." *Physica D: Nonlinear Phenomena* 224, no. 1 (January 1, 2006): 202–212. doi:10.1016/j.physd.2006.09.008.

Zhu, Xueling, Xiang Wang, Jin Xiao, Jian Liao, Mingtian Zhong, Wei Wang, and Shuqiao Yao. "Evidence of a Dissociation Pattern in Resting-State Default Mode Network Connectivity in First-Episode, Treatment-Naive Major Depression Patients." *Biological Psychiatry* 71, no. 7 (April 2012): 611–617. doi:10.1016/j.biopsych.2011.10.035.

Zuo, Xi-Nian, Adriana Di Martino, Clare Kelly, Zarrar E. Shehzad, Dylan G. Gee, Donald F. Klein, F. Xavier Castellanos, Bharat B. Biswal, and Michael P. Milham. "The Oscillating Brain: Complex and Reliable." *NeuroImage* 49, no. 2 (January 15, 2010): 1432–1445. doi:10.1016/j.neuroimage.2009.09.037.

O/R

Are you interested in reading more from one of the liveliest independent publishers working today? See our entire list at www.orbooks.com.

Consider buying direct from OR, and take advantage of our special web-only discounts: it's better for you, our authors—and us as well.